PUBLISH,
Don't Perish

PUBLISH, Don't Perish

The Scholar's Guide to Academic Writing and Publishing

JOSEPH M. MOXLEY

Foreword by Robert Boice

Released from
Samford University Library

 PRAEGER

Westport, Connecticut
London

Samford University Library

Library of Congress Cataloging-in-Publication Data

Moxley, Joseph Michael.
    Publish, don't perish : the scholar's guide to academic writing
  and publishing / Joseph M. Moxley ; foreword by Robert Boice.
      p.   cm.
  Includes bibliographical references (p.   ) and index.
  ISBN 0–275–94453–0 (pb. : alk. paper)
    1. Scholarly publishing.   2. Learning and scholarship—Authorship.
  3. College teachers as authors.   4. Authors and publishers.
  I. Title.
  Z286.S37M7   1992b
  070.5—dc20   92–22639

British Library Cataloguing in Publication Data is available.

Copyright © 1992 by Joseph M. Moxley

All rights reserved. No portion of this book may be
reproduced, by any process or technique, without the
express written consent of the publisher.

A hardcover edition of *Publish, Don't Perish* is available from Greenwood Press, an
imprint of Greenwood Publishing Group, Inc. (ISBN: 0-313-27735-4).

Library of Congress Catalog Card Number: 92–22639
ISBN: 0-275-94453-0

First published in 1992

Praeger Publishers, 88 Post Road West, Westport, CT 06881
An imprint of Greenwood Publishing Group, Inc.

Printed in the United States of America

The paper used in this book complies with the
Permanent Paper standard issued by the National
Information Standards Organization (Z39.48-1984).

10 9 8 7 6 5 4 3 2 1

Z
286
.S37
M7
1992b

for
Craig Joseph Moxley

Contents

Foreword

In a way, this book represents an other brother. Consider a classic parallel. Alexander von Humboldt remains famous for his scientific discoveries, including the ocean current that bears his name. His brother William, despite having deeply affected German and American universities, is generally forgotten. It was he, as state minister of education and organizer of the University of Berlin (1810), who set the precedent for hiring professors more on the basis of their skills as researchers than as teachers.

The irony in this far-reaching decision is that for all the complaints it continues to elicit, we have neglected to study its effects in systematic fashion. We still do not really know if involvement in research and scholarship impedes teaching. And we still have a sketchy record of helping professors thrive as writers. So it is that we know far more about the reasons why some writers procrastinated (say, the mathematician Gauss, a contemporary of the von Humboldt brothers) than about why others wrote fluently (say, Voltaire).

Consider a more recent analogue. In the modern discipline of faculty development, support for professorial writing remains on the margin—as the other brother. As a rule, programs for faculty are run by instructional development specialists whose efforts omit help with writing and publishing. Titles of the most beloved books in faculty development tell the story of exclusion: *Turning Professors into Teachers* (Joseph Katz, Macmillan), *Teaching Tips* (William McKeachie, Heath), *Improving College Teaching* (Maryellen Weimer, Jossey-Bass). Even the cutting-edge serial in the area excludes assistance in scholarship and publishing: *New Directions for Teaching and Learning*. And, to complete this brief overview, books about higher education generally relegate research and writing to villainous roles as underminers of teaching (e.g., Page Smith's *Killing the Spirit*, Viking). Academic writing, for all its supposed importance to survival in professorial careers, has gotten little favorable or useful press, Still, there is promise.

Consider my own experiences in faculty development as an example of the marginalized but improving status accorded to support programs for scholarly writing. Two decades ago I was apparently one of the first academics to travel from campus to campus with workshops for professors as writers. The instructional developers who shared in the responsibility for recruiting me were often ambivalent ("I hope this won't give the wrong message about how much we value teaching here") and skeptical ("I doubt that we'll get more than a handful of faculty to attend; our people already know how to write"). Their colleagues, however, enthusiastically oversubscribed workshops; the faculty had no doubts about their potential helpfulness. My own surveys conducted as I came to these campuses suggested that some 60 to 80 percent of their faculty were writing and publishing far less than they considered minimally desirable. The same respondents saw their silence, discomfort, and invisibility as primary disappointments. Faculty developers, once they saw the need for writing supports, grew more accepting of the idea.

In the national organization for faculty developers, POD (Professional and Organizational Development Network), nurturance for writing is also finding an overdue acceptance. A decade ago, POD simply diverted my proposals for conference papers.

Five years later, ambivalence had replaced rejection (reviewers asked, "Is this really faculty development; would it be a disservice to sanction it?"). Only a year ago, I was asked to conduct a preconference POD workshop on managing scholarly writing amid busy schedules for faculty developers; it was well attended and well received. In that same year, I finally got past the gatekeepers of higher education journals with a manuscript reporting my long-term studies of faculty need for help with research and writing. The results of those repeated interviews and observations are relevant here. While we might readily suppose that new hires come to campus without proper grounding as teachers, my studies indicate similar deficits in managing writing and publishing. Not only did new faculty fail to find time, support, and ideas for writing; they often lacked a clear conception of how to format and prepare manuscripts for publication. Sadly, the new faculty most in peril of failing as writers and as professors were women and minorities.

What fosters this change in the acceptability of addressing needs for help with writing? As academe persists in democratizing and diversifying its faculty, perhaps it sees the need to protect its investments with support programs that include aid for writing and publishing. And, while their colleagues seemed to pause, feminists such as Sandra Scarr took the lead in sharing the secrets of academic productivity and visibility—the tacit knowledge transmitted more selectively by old boy networks. In my recent travels, I see another hint of promise. Most campuses now have one or more designated professors assuming increasing responsibility for assisting colleagues with writing and publishing.

There are commonalities among these new kinds of faculty developers. They tend to be younger rather than older. They bring a record of productivity and a sense of enthusiasm to the endeavor. And they openly share practical intelligence about thriving as academic writers, often by assembling and sharing the experience of other successful and altruistic colleagues. Without fail, in my observations, their services meet with heavy and appreciative demand. This is where the present book, *Publish, Don't Perish,* comes in. At last the thawing has produced a tried and published compilation of the kinds of advice and direction being disseminated on some campuses. Here, as the inevitable next step in that increasing flow, is a thorough-going alternative to the information being independently (and inefficiently) reassembled across colleges and universities.

Consider, finally, what the author of *Publish, Don't Perish*, Joe Moxley, offers that is especially promising. First of all, he prescribes simple and practical strategies for academic writers (e.g., prewriting schemes for searching the literature; organizational devices such as free-written drafts; guidelines for generating ideas such as a double-entry system of note keeping that encourages writers to dialogue with what they are reading). Second, he debunks myths that can stymie writers (e.g., beliefs that writers always enjoy writing, that gifted scholars criticize their work during its formative stages). Third, he outlines the activities that campuses and professional organizations must address if the 85 to 90 percent of usually silent faculty members are to stand up publicly and say "This is who I am" in print (e.g., he points out that institutions must attend as much to quality as to quantity of scholarly writing; that journals must help humanize the peer-review system). Finally, Joe Moxley models and explains the basics of composition theory/practice in ways that promote effective organization, writing, and editing. As an award-winning teacher of writing, an insightful theorist in composition, and a widely published writer, he does all of these things with compelling ease. In the end, Joe Moxley offers just the sort of exemplar essential to credibility in a topic traditionally kept in the backwaters.

Robert Boice
Stony Brook, New York

Acknowledgments

I am particularly indebted to the University of South Florida for offering me a sabbatical so that I could write this book and complete several other projects. I owe a special debt of gratitude to Marilyn Brownstein at Greenwood Press for encouraging me to write this book, to Barbara Goodhouse for her careful copyediting, and to Nita Romer for her work on the book's design. In addition, I thank Lagretta Lenker at the Division of Lifelong Learning and Provost G. G. Meisels for their unflagging support of my workshops with university faculty. Finally, I thank my wife, Pat Hemmens Moxley, for her continued support.

Introduction

At first glance academic publishing appears to be a healthy, thriving enterprise. In the sciences alone, it has been estimated that "two journal articles are published every minute" (Coughlin A4). Since the 1900s, "only 2–3 percent of all manuscripts make it into book form" (Aronowitz 44; Parsons 51). Because university presses, journals, and trade-book publishers reject manuscripts by the ton, it may seem logical to assume that too much emphasis is placed on publishing in academia. With thousands of pages being printed each day, scholars appear to be having a difficult time even reading each other's work. In a survey of "papers published in 1984 and the citations they accumulated through 1988" of a database that included 10 percent of all scientific journals published worldwide, David Pendlebury found that few scholars are citing each other's work: physics has about 37 percent uncited, medicine 46 percent, mathematics 55 percent, engineering 72 percent, and social sciences 74 percent (Hamilton 25). Perhaps, as numerous critics have contended, scholars do not read other scholars' work because so much of it is poorly written. Or perhaps scholarship should take a back seat to teaching. Perhaps the critics are right: maybe we should worry more about preserving the Canadian forests than publishing academic monographs.

In truth, however, a much stronger argument can be made for the opposite case: *academicians are not publishing enough.* While this argument may seem spurious in light of the avalanche of manuscripts publishers receive, we can find convincing support for it. First, research suggests that the bulk of scholarship is produced by a relatively small number of scholars: only about 10 to 20 percent of our colleagues appear to be responsible for the bulk of what is published (Jalongo; Boyer; Sykes). In "Why Academicians Don't Write," Robert Boice and Ferdinand Jones conclude: "The median number of scholarly publications for even the most prolific disciplines like psychology is zero. Most academicians who do write contribute infrequently; as few as 10 percent of writers in specific areas account for over 50 percent of the literature" (568). Strangely, as Boice and Jones point out in their review article, we have failed to question why so few of us write and publish our ideas. Before assuming that too much publishing is occurring, we should consider the implications of having most of the scholarship produced by a limited number of scholars, many of them relatively inexperienced junior faculty writing to gain tenure. Although academicians' careers are often controlled by what they publish, few researchers have questioned how editorial decisions are made, how academicians write, or how academic literature is used.

While scholars have been silent about how they develop and publish ideas, most institutions and professional organizations have failed to provide guidance or support for scholarly publishing. Few institutions provide workshops in writing and marketing scholarly manuscripts. As a result, some academicians are unaware of prewriting, revising, and editing strategies. Because our culture tends to mystify and aggrandize the creative process, many academicians are unaware of how productive authors work. They are often naïve about how politics and subjective factors taint the editorial process. Many academicians are unaware of the aggressive marketing strategies they may need to publish their work. Instead of providing a helping hand, the implicit message that scholars, institutions, and professional organizations give about scholarly publishing is sink or swim, publish or perish.

Yet, we should seriously question what would happen if more academicians published. *Perhaps the educational crisis facing Americans would be diminished if we encouraged greater participation.* This may seem like an extreme statement, yet let us recall whom we are talking about—the professoriate, leading experts in their disciplines. After all, silence does not necessarily correlate with a lack of originality. If we involve more than 10 percent of the professoriate in scholarly publishing, we could hope for solutions to some of the major problems confronting our society. With more contributions being made by some of our country's brightest people, we could hope for longer, healthier lives. Perhaps medical researchers could find a cure for AIDS, environmental scientists could stop global warming, engineers and physicists could develop a cheap alternative to petroleum. If professors read and wrote more, we would probably see major transformations in what books are assigned and published and in what research methods are deemed appropriate. Nonpublishing instructors could cast off their role as *technicians* and become *producers of knowledge.* Insightful students who are mimicking our behaviors would see that learning and education are ongoing processes, that publishing scholarship promotes intellectual invigoration.

While this conjecture may seem exaggerated, it is actually based on one of the firmest findings of researchers in the field of composition and rhetoric: *writing is a generative, thought-provoking process.* We don't sit down and record our thoughts. Instead, we often discover our most inspired ideas when writing. Sometimes our clumsiest, weakest beginnings evolve, surprisingly, into our most elegant introductions. A day when we feel sluggish and lackluster can suddenly become one of our most inspired days.

Because writing promotes original thought, we can expect encouraging more scholars to participate in scholarly writing to result in more innovative thinking. If more academicians wrote, we could expect breakthroughs in scientific and humanistic disciplines. Once scholars gain momentum, sentences bump against each other and make us ask "Why?" and "So what?" This questioning process can spark revelations that ignite our passion and curiosity. For just as we know that gravity exists, so do we know that innovative ideas occur when our sentences and paragraphs bump into each other, causing us to rethink assumptions and observations.

HOW CAN THIS BOOK HELP YOU PUBLISH SCHOLARLY DOCUMENTS?

In this book I offer suggestions for developing, polishing, and publishing scholarly ideas based on my own experience as an academic writer, on composition theory and research, and on the recommendations of colleagues who have enrolled in the scholarly writing workshops that I have been teaching at the University of South Florida since the fall of 1988. My hope is that this book will help you publish ideas that are important to you and to the members of your discipline. Ultimately, as I argue more fully in the concluding chapter of this book, I hope that institutions, professional organizations, and scholars can work together to reconsider what constitutes scholarship, to reject the arbitrary wedge between scholarship and teaching, and to provide more information about composing and marketing strategies.

While I have attempted to write a practical how-to book, I have also addressed the politics and problems of scholarly publishing. For instance, instead of saying, "Here's how to write a book review: a, b, c," I have also explained why it may not be in your best interests to write book reviews. While my perspective is inevitably shaped by my work in composition and rhetoric, I have tried to incorporate comments made by colleagues in other disciplines.

I have deliberately written short chapters so that you can easily find what you need. Part I provides an overview of the working habits and attitudes of successful academic writers. In the early stages of composing, I encourage you to play the *believing game—*

that is, to have faith that inchoate ideas will find form and substance through drafting. If you have trouble finding time to write or if you are unsure about how to develop scholarly projects, chapters 1 through 4 should be especially useful to you. Chapter 5 provides marketing techniques and examines the politics and editorial policies of scholarly publishing.

Part II analyzes the conventions of various scholarly genres, such as abstracts, introductions, conclusions, book reviews, quantitative and qualitative research articles, book proposals, and grant proposals. While the opening chapters encourage authors to play the believing game when composing the early drafts, Part III explains how to play the *doubting game*—how to attack your manuscript as your critics do. Chapter 16 reviews the critical questions that readers are likely to ask when evaluating your documents. In turn, Chapter 17 offers editorial strategies for making your sentences economical, precise, and concise.

In the concluding chapter—"Where Can We Go from Here?"—I address the critics of higher education who have accused us of abandoning the classroom. In particular, I critique how we have defined scholarship and driven an arbitrary wedge between teaching and research. Finally, I outline changes that institutions, professional organizations, and scholars need to make in order to motivate faculty to engage in scholarly writing and publishing.

WORKS CITED

Aronowitz, Stanley. "A Writer's Union for Academics?" *Thought and Action: The NEA Higher Education Journal* 4:2 (Fall 1988): 41–46.

Boice, Robert, and Ferdinand Jones. "Why Academicians Don't Write." *Journal of Higher Education* 55 (September/October 1984): 567–582.

Boyer, Ernst. Quoted in "The New York Times Education Summer Survey." *New York Times*, 18 August 1985: 36.

Coughlin, Ellen. "Concerns about Fraud, Editorial Bias Prompt Scrutiny of Journal Practices." *Chronicle of Higher Education*, 15 February 1989: A4–A7.

Hamilton, David P. "Research Papers: Who's Uncited Now?" *Science* 251 (January 1991): 25.

Jalongo, Mary Renck. "Faculty Productivity in Higher Education." *Educational Forum* 49 (Winter 1985): 171–182.

Parsons, Paul. *Getting Published: The Acquisition Process at University Presses.* Knoxville: University of Tennessee Press, 1989.

Sykes, Charles J. *ProfScam: Professors and the Demise of Higher Education.* Washington, D.C.: Regnery Gateway, 1988.

Part I

How to Get Started

1

What Myths Interfere with Your Scholarship?

From my workshops with academicians, I know that professors are often skeptical about discussing how they compose manuscripts or how they market their work. Because they have so many demands placed on them and have such little time to improve as writers, they often want a quick fix—a sure-fire formula for writing well. As a result, my colleagues are typically pleased when I review the revising and editing strategies that are discussed in Part III of this book.

However, knowledge of how journal and book editors critique manuscripts cannot help professors produce these manuscripts. To become effective at generating original ideas, professors need to analyze myths about how writers generate, critique, and publish ideas. By becoming more aware of the working habits and attitudes of other writers, professors can reject myths about the writing process that interfere with their ability to develop ideas. Below I critique some of the most prevalent myths about composing and academic scholarship that keep many of us from realizing our potential as writers and scholars.

SCHOLARSHIP INTERFERES WITH TEACHING

Reality: Because many academicians at research universities feel that teaching well is not rewarded, they tend to assume that the emphasis on conducting original research is to blame. After all, they argue, time spent researching and publishing is time taken away from grading papers and conferencing with students. Yet since academicians at research institutions are offered course-load releases for conducting research, we truly have no reason to assume that conducting research is pernicious to scholarship. Instead, we actually have convincing evidence that scholarship can result in better teaching. As Mary Jalongo has pointed out in her comprehensive review of literature, scholarship and teaching involve similar skills: "creativity, perceptivity, decision-making, and spontaneity" as well as "originality, thoughtful interpretation, sensitivity to audience, impact on readers, and technical accuracy" (49). In addition, Jalongo identifies four primary ways that scholarly publishing can help teaching:

1. *Sphere of influence*: Faculty members do not write to reach only the students or colleagues within the sound of their own voices. Through publication, the scholar-teacher's influence extends beyond the confines of a classroom, to students in other classes and in other institutions, and potentially to everywhere with a bookstore or library. . . .

2. *Teaching materials*: Often faculty members' writings are directly related to course content and can be used to support lectures. . . . Their authors' best thinking on a topic is neatly typeset. As a result, teacher-authors are free to use a wider variety of instructional strategies because at least some of the course material—their own—is pre-packaged.

3. *Knowledge of field*: Writing develops a deeper level of understanding about one's field. . . . Writing also forces instructors to rehearse ideas and effective ways of presenting them. Thinking long and hard, going through the composing process, experiencing the rigors of peer review—all these efforts enable scholar-teachers to anticipate the questions of students and answer them meaningfully.

4. *Scholarly role*: According to Maslow, self-actualization is built upon fulfillment of the needs for belongingness and for esteem. Successful scholar-teachers are more likely to have these needs met than their unpublished peers. Faculty members who are productive authors believe that they belong in a community of scholars. (55)

While noting the argument that publishing faculty may have less time to meet individually with students than faculty who merely teach, Jalongo further observes, "It is still possible to confuse quantity of time with quality of time. Surely a well-focused twenty minutes with a brilliant scholar can be more beneficial than a lengthy contact with a lackluster faculty member" (54).

In his research into why academicians write, Robert Boice determined that publishing scholars often receive higher teaching evaluations than nonpublishers. Boice speculates that the publishing scholars in his study may have received higher evaluations because they did not overprepare and "were less pressured to present as much lecture material and more likely to involve students as active learners" ("Strategies" 23).[1]

As I argue in more detail in the concluding chapter of this book, we need to reassert teaching as a significant form of scholarship, as a way of synthesizing and extending knowledge. Yet we need to be careful not to think dualistically—that is, to assume that teaching and scholarship are contrary elements like oil and water that can only work well by being shaken vigorously together.

ACADEMIC PUBLISHING IS A GENTEEL PROFESSION, CARRIED ON BY SCHOLARS WITHOUT CONCERN FOR MARKET CONSIDERATIONS

Reality: Sure, editors want to advance knowledge. They hope to redefine a discipline by publishing works that question conventions and assumptions. And some editors even hope to shape society by educating readers. Yet scholarly publishing *is* a business that is sensitive to the same market considerations as other businesses. The bottom line is that editors must publish what their readerships want. Yes, a few well-endowed university presses can publish an occasional project that they don't expect to pay the electric bill. By and large, however, editors need to evaluate ideas from the perspective of their intended readers. Even the well-established presses are backing away from projects that will not sell at least 2,000 copies. For example, Walter Lippincott, the current director of Princeton University Press, wants to do away with "the prestigious sixteen-year-old Princeton Series of Contemporary Poets" because poetry is not selling well, regardless of quality: "Basically, the sales were so terrible. . . . If we can't get more than 700 readers for paperbacks priced under $10, in some cases, then it may not be worth doing at all" ("Inside Publishing" 11).

WRITERS ARE UNUSUAL, ESPECIALLY INTELLIGENT PEOPLE

Reality: Perhaps a few people are born with a special drive and ability to express themselves via language. Yet ability without desire or experience nets an empty page. Despite countless attempts, researchers have been unable to prove that writers are uniquely intelligent or original. What we can say, however, is that writers *discipline* themselves to write and revise. When their thoughts remain muddy, successful writers persist until they achieve clarity.

WRITERS ALWAYS ENJOY WRITING[2]

Reality: Many of the faculty members with whom I have worked over the years have been reluctant to admit that they dislike writing. Sometimes scientists and doctors dislike writing because they have not done much of it or because they are not as adroit with language as with mathematical symbols. For many of us, the urge to write is thwarted by memories of mean-spirited teachers who never said anything good about our writing (Boice, *Professors*). In fact, studies of teachers' methods of responding to student writing have determined that English teachers seldom comment positively on student papers (Moxley). When admonished to publish or perish, it's easy to understand why we can perceive academic writing as an onerous activity. Many of us chose academia so that we could be our own boss.

While we can hope that more people would enjoy writing if it were taught differently, we should also note that many accomplished, professional writers agonize about their writing from time to time. Consider, for example, the following admission from Sue Lorch, a well-published English professor:

I do not like to write. Most people to whom I reveal this small, personal truth find it exceedingly odd, suggesting by their expressions that I ought either to repair my attitude or develop the discretion necessary not to go around telling people about it. Apparently these people hear my confession as an admission of fraud. Because my professional life centers on the written word—on producing it, interpreting it, teaching it, and teaching others to teach it, people assume that I should enjoy writing. Not at all. I inevitably view the prospect of writing with a mental set more commonly reserved for root canals and amputations: If it must be done, it must be done, but for God's sake, let us put it off as long as possible. (165)

GIFTED SCHOLARS ARE OVERFLOWING WITH IDEAS; THEY NEED MERELY LOOK INWARD TO DISCOVER ORIGINAL IDEAS

Reality: In his lectures delivered at the University of Tokyo between 1896 and 1902, Lafcadio Hearn made the following observation:

> Nothing has been more productive of injury to young literary students than those stories, or legends, about great writers having written great books in a very short time. They suggest what must be in a million cases impossible, as a common possibility. . . . It is much more valuable to remember that Gray passed fourteen years in correcting and improving a single poem, and that no great poem or book, as we now have the text, represents the first form of the text. . . . Almost everything composed by Tennyson was changed and changed again, to such an extent that in almost every edition the text differed. Above all things do not imagine that any good work can be done without immense pains. (45–46)

Unfortunately, to this day composition theorists are still fighting the fantasy that great authors wait to write until they are inspired. For while it is true that some authors can compose perfect first drafts, this approach is the exception, not the rule. Like most other people, accomplished writers have long, weary days. Even on the worst days, however, they have faith in the creative process; their experience tells them that the chaos and frustration of early drafting will subside once a few drafts are written. Also, they look outside of themselves for ideas by reading extensively, observing their world, and speaking with people.

In his extensive research of professors as writers, Robert Boice has determined that regular writing promotes creativity (*Professors*). By challenging themselves to write thirty minutes a day, five days a week, Boice has found that academicians can write several essays a year. Boice's research in which professors suffered negative consequences for not writing has helped us reaffirm what professional writers have said throughout the centuries: regular writing promotes creativity ("Neglected").

GIFTED SCHOLARS ARE CRITICAL OF THEIR WORK WHEN THEY ARE PLANNING AND DRAFTING THEIR IDEAS

Reality: When they are just beginning a writing project, experienced writers ignore doubts about the quality of their ideas. They understand that they cannot evaluate the originality of an idea based on a first or second draft. They often ignore questions about how best to organize their ideas or whether or not their rough drafts contain grammatical and mechanical errors.

GIFTED WRITERS KNOW WHAT THEY WILL WRITE ABOUT BEFORE WRITING

Reality: While you may occasionally know what you want to say before writing, much scholarship involves giving form to new ideas. In fact, much of the frustration as well as the joy that scholars express about writing relates to the Eureka Phenomenon—the energized sensation that one feels when a new insight shatters previous ideas:

> *Think before you speak is criticism's motto; speak before you think is creation's.* —E. M. Forster
> *I write because I don't know what I think until I read what I have to say.* —Flannery O'Connor
> *You write—and find you have something to say.*
> —Wright Morris
> *Creation must take place between the pen and the paper, not before in a thought or afterwards in a recasting.*
> —Gertrude Stein
> *But I really write to find out what I know about something and what is to be known about something. . . . I write books to find out about things.* —Dame Rebecca West

WRITING SHOULD BE A LONELY CRAFT CONDUCTED BY INTROVERTS

Reality: Scholarly writing is an inherently social activity. We join in the conversation of our peers by being knowledgeable of the important discussions taking place in our disciplines. The myth of the lonely writer in the garret ignores the inherently social nature of writing. Writing need not be a solitary, lonely act. In fact, writers who do not enjoy working in isolation can either coauthor documents or arrange to meet with friends and write on their separate subjects. Others find it useful to write in noisy college cafeterias. And even if you do your best writing in a quiet room away from other people, you can probably do your best revising by observing how your words influence actual readers. When you can no longer find fault with your manuscript, there's nothing better to reinvigorate yourself and to find errors than to share it with trusted colleagues.

WRITERS WORK BEST SITTING ALONE AT THEIR DESKS

Reality: Your best ideas may not occur when you are sitting at your desk. If you are receptive, sudden insights may arrive when you are bustling about in the world, playing golf, or driving in busy traffic. Studies of the creative processes of scientists and artists suggest that their most innovative breakthroughs transpire during slack moments between work and play, so you may find it useful to keep a note pad or tape recorder handy.

QUALITY WRITING IS ALWAYS DEVELOPED SPONTANEOUSLY: TRULY SKILLED WRITERS RARELY REVISE

Reality: Professional writers perceive revision not as a process of correcting errors, but as a way of developing and discovering their ideas. Interviews and studies of working writers have determined that most people depend on revision to transform inchoate, underdeveloped phrases into elegant sentences, paragraphs, and books.

ONCE WRITTEN, THE WORD IS FINAL

Reality: Sure, when you submit your manuscripts for publication, you should believe in what you have said. Ideally, your published works represent your best thinking on a subject. However, you should also feel free to change your mind when reviewing your work at a later date. Productive scholars recognize that thinking is an ongoing process. Rigid thinkers, like rigid writers, are characterized by bitterness and sarcasm, failing to be invigorated by an ever-changing world.

ACADEMIC AUTHORS SHOULD ESCHEW THE FIRST PERSON AND AVOID REVEALING PERSONAL EXPERIENCES IN THEIR WRITING

Reality: The ludicrous assumption that scholars can be more objective by avoiding the first person contributes significantly to poor writing. Readability experts and writing stylists have mourned the death of the first person for decades.[3]

THE PEER-REVIEW PROCESS IS FAIR AND OBJECTIVE

Reality: Although criticisms of the peer-review process are common, professional organizations and researchers have failed to investigate thoroughly the efficacy of existing approaches or alternatives. Nevertheless, the little research that has been done suggests that the peer-review system is seriously troubled. After examining "402 reviews of 153 papers submitted to 12 editors of American Psychological Association journals," Douglas Fiske and Louis Fogg concluded: "In the typical case, two reviews of the same paper had no critical point in common. It seemed that reviewers did not overtly disagree on particular points; instead, they wrote about different topics, each making points that were appropriate and accurate. As a consequence, their recommendations about editorial decisions showed hardly any agreement" (591). After examining the 3,477 weaknesses identified in the 402 reviews of 153 articles, Fiske and Fogg were impressed by the "amount of time and effort that reviewers put into their work." For scholars desperate to keep their jobs and feed their families, the diversity of the reviewers' commentaries is more than troublesome. If some readers tend to focus on the research design, others on statistical analyses, and others on the writing style, how can an author anticipate all of the possible criticisms? If another 402 reviews were solicited, could we expect 3,477 more weaknesses to be identified? Fiske and Fogg wisely encourage prospective authors to solicit criticisms of articles from colleagues before submitting them, yet even this strategy cannot prepare an author for the inherently subjective nature of the peer-review process.

The research conducted by Douglas P. Peters of the University of North Dakota and Stephen J. Ceci of Cornell University provides an even stronger condemnation of the peer-review system. To determine whether essays are carefully read by reviewers in the sciences, Peters and Ceci selected twelve articles that had been published by professors from prestigious universities. They changed the authors' names and downgraded the prestige of their affiliations, then resubmitted the articles to the same periodicals that had originally published them. Surprisingly, although thirty-eight editors and peer reviewers considered the resubmissions, only three of the essays were identified as having already been published. Of the remaining nine articles resubmitted to the peer review process, only one was accepted for publication. The other eight articles were rejected for "serious methodological flaws" (Coughlin).[4]

Because editors try to bolster the prestige of their journals by accepting manuscripts from prestigious authors and institutions, a built-in elitist factor appears to determine what manuscripts are accepted. Because of this, some journals are beginning to require that authors not mention their names or affiliations in their manuscripts.

John W. Kronik, editor of the Modern Language Association's *PMLA*, has reported that since blind submissions were started in 1980 for *PMLA*, "quite suddenly and drastically, we find that, among the articles printed, there has been a significant increase in articles by women, by junior members of the profession, and by colleagues from lesser institutions" (Coughlin A7).

EVERYONE SHOULD WRITE IN ROUGHLY THE SAME WAY

Reality: Each rhetorical situation—that is, different audiences and purposes—will strongly affect how you compose. In addition, we all have various idiosyncratic ways of "priming the pump." Thus, some writers may need to exercise before they write, while others need to sit quietly in the library. Instead of attempting to produce all manuscripts in the same way, try to be as flexible as possible. It may take you thirty drafts to complete a document, or you may write a perfect first draft. Sometimes you may want to dictate, at other times work on the computer, and at other times write with a pencil.

NOTES

1. Boice's conclusions raise an interesting question for future research: Does the questioning stance of the researcher more successfully model the role of the active learner than that of the professor as the holder and dispenser of knowledge?

2. If you particularly dislike writing, you may find it useful to try some of the self-reflexive writing exercises described in Chapter 4. Composition theorists and psychologists have found that writing about why we are blocked can help us gain momentum, solve writing problems, and discover publishable topics.

3. See Chapter 17 for a more complete discussion of why the first person is often preferable to passive or third-person constructions.

4. Interestingly, Peters and Ceci had great difficulty publishing their study. Before being accepted by the *Behavioral and Brain Sciences*, it was rejected by *Science* and by the *American Psychologist*. According to a recent essay by Michael Mahoney in the *Journal of Social Behavior and Personality*, Peters and

Ceci have been ostracized by the scientific community and have lost " 'indirect' support (secretarial assistance, photocopying, postage)" for their continued scholarship (124).

WORKS CITED

Boice, Robert. "The Neglected Third Factor in Writing: Productivity." *College Composition and Communication* 36 (December 1985): 472–479.

———. *Professors as Writers*. Stillwater, Okla.: New Forums Press, 1990.

———. "Strategies for Enhancing Scholarly Productivity." In *Writing and Publishing for Academic Authors*. Ed. Joseph M. Moxley. Lanham, Md.: University Press of America, 1992. 15–32.

Coughlin, Ellen. "Concerns about Fraud, Editorial Bias Prompt Scrutiny of Journal Practices." *Chronicle of Higher Education*, 15 February 1989: A4–A7.

Fiske, Donald W., and Louis Fogg. "But the Reviewers Are Making Different Criticisms of My Paper!" *American Psychologist* (May 1990): 591–598.

Hearn, Lafcadio. *Life and Literature*. New York: Dodd, Mead, 1929.

"Inside Publishing." *Lingua Franca* (April 1991): 11–15.

Jalongo, Mary Renck. "On the Compatibility of Teaching and Scholarly Writing." *Scholarly Publishing* (October 1987): 49–58.

Lorch, Sue. "Confessions of a Former Sailor." In *Writers on Writing*. Ed. Tom Waldrep. New York: Random House, 1985. 165–172.

Moxley, Joseph M. "Responding to Student Writing: Goals, Methods, Alternatives." *Freshman English News* 17 (Spring 1989): 3–4, 9–14.

Sykes, Charles J. *ProfScam: Professors and the Demise of Higher Education*. Washington, D.C.: Regnery Gateway, 1988.

2

How to Develop Scholarly Projects

The path from the desire to write, to the original idea, and then to publication is often fraught with chaos, feelings of self doubt, error, and frustration. This is why it's often said that it's easier to critique than to invent. Few academicians can write a perfect first draft. Most of us require some time to wander around our offices, sharpen pencils, clean our homes, or browse through current periodicals. More precisely, most of us need some *prewriting time*—time to read more deeply about a subject, time for planning a research design, time for discussing ideas with colleagues. Prewriting also involves analyzing the *rhetorical situation* for a document, which we can do by asking numerous questions, such as "Who is my *audience*? What is my *purpose*? What *voice* do I hope to project?"

While simple subjects may require little prewriting, most academic works require extensive prewriting. If you fail to give some careful thought to your rhetorical context, schedule, and goals at the onset of a scholarly project, you may find two years down the line that the audience for your project is too small to warrant publication, or that others have already done what you have set out to do, or that the methodology is severely flawed. Of course there are tremendous advantages to writing to discover ideas and form, yet you also must be practical—plan your time so you do not waste it!

The writing strategies discussed in this chapter are designed to help shatter writing blocks and develop more polished first drafts, thereby reducing needless revisions:

1. Become aware of the important conversations occurring in your discipline.

2. Consider collaborating with a colleague (or colleagues).

3. Analyze the economic and political constraints that impinge on how you write.

4. Analyze your schedule, break the manuscript into manageable sections, and establish due dates for first, second, and subsequent drafts.

5. Analyze the rhetorical situation for the document.

BECOME AWARE OF THE IMPORTANT CONVERSATIONS OCCURRING IN YOUR DISCIPLINE

Within the past few years, we have become increasingly aware of the inherently social and collaborative nature of academic publishing. Understandably, we all differ in how social we care to be, but the bottom line is that what constitutes a significant contribution to the literature is often determined by what scholarly conversations are taking place, by what's fashionable and what's not. Instead of hiding away in a garret or basement lab, many academicians try to learn as much as possible about the various conversations in their disciplines. They can do this by reading assiduously; by attending conferences; by serving on professional committees; by serving as reviewers of journal articles, academic books, grants, and textbooks; by studying reviewers' comments to submitted work; and by getting to know editors on a first-name basis.

Do a Comprehensive Search of Available Literature

Little is more disheartening than finding that the essay you have spent four months writing has already been written and published by someone else. To ensure that you are not reinventing the wheel, you should conduct a thorough investigation of the literature.

The most comprehensive and efficient way to review existing literature on a topic is to do a computerized search. Essentially, via computer modems, you have over 500 on-line indexes to choose from that can put you in touch with countless essays, books, pamphlets, and statistics. Also, many research libraries have CD-ROM (compact disc-read only memory) indexes available, which work much like on-line databases except that the information is stored on CDs. The primary advantage of the CD-ROM and on-line databases over traditional printed indexes is that they allow you to sift through thousands of essays in minutes. In addition to providing the full bibliographic citation for published materials, many computerized databases offer abstracts for indexed articles, which enable you to determine whether a particular source will be useful. A few of the databases, such as the *Social Science Citation Index*, allow you to determine how many times a particular document has been quoted by other scholars. Within seconds you can also take a look at each of the references provided in a bibliography and then access these sources to determine whether they will be useful. Some CD-ROM databases allow you to save the contents of a search on a floppy disc so that the user can review the search at home on an IBM or IBM-compatible computer.

Although searching procedures differ, most databases use the same vocabulary of *subject descriptors* as those provided in *The Library of Congress Subject Headings*. To determine which descriptors you should use to conduct your search, consult with a reference librarian or review *Online Searching: A Dictionary and Bibliographic Guide*, which offers a glossary of descriptors that are now used by on-line and CD-ROM databases.

Even if a computer search uncovers investigations similar to yours, you should not necessarily give up hope on your project.

Because the act of writing generates new ideas, you can expect your ideas to gain forcefulness, maybe even elegance, with rewriting. Consequently, don't immediately give up on a subject if others have already addressed it. In short, follow your instinct, yet proceed with caution.

Talk with Colleagues about Your Subject

Some academicians are reluctant to share their ideas with editors and colleagues. In part, this reluctance is a realistic response to those inconsiderate people who presents others' ideas as their own. Yet the benefits of working collaboratively far exceed the risks. Your colleagues can be invaluable sources of support and inspiration; the ideas you generate with them can far exceed those you could develop by yourself. If you sense that intradepartmental rivalries will interfere with and taint any attempt to establish a community of scholars and authors, you may want to look outside your department. Colleagues at your home institution in a different department who are willing to read your work can motivate you to get the work done and can help you eliminate unnecessary jargon. By attending professional conferences, you can meet colleagues at other universities who are energized by your ideas and willing to exchange criticisms on manuscripts.

CONSIDER COLLABORATING WITH A COLLEAGUE (OR COLLEAGUES)

Coauthoring manuscripts can be highly rewarding. On the best of occasions, we can develop ideas collectively that are much stronger than any we could develop on our own. Developing professional friendships, discussing possibilities, seeing how others write, having your manuscripts revised by a trusted colleague, learning new research techniques—these are some of the important benefits of collaboration. Yet colleagues can fail to fulfill their obligations. If they are busy working on other projects, if their professional work isn't all that significant to them, or if they are going through some sort of life crisis, they can miss deadlines or produce shoddy work, requiring extra effort on your part.

Before agreeing to coauthor a manuscript, give some thought to how you and your coauthor (or coauthors) will work together and how your work will be evaluated by your institution. If you don't feel comfortable sitting down with your colleague and mapping out a schedule of duties and goals, then your project may quickly roll into the Twilight Zone of Group Think in which no one makes their best effort and no deadlines are ever met. While at the onset of a project you may be unable to delineate all of the necessary tasks, you should at least be able to agree in principle to the amount of time each colleague will give to the project, whether contributors will be equal or unequal in the amount of time expected of them, and whether authors' names will be listed alphabetically, according to the amount of their contribution, according to their respective ranks, or according to the toss of a coin. You may want to consider the following questions[1] before deciding to coauthor a project:

1. Do I like the prospective colleague? Do I want to spend time with this person?

2. Can the colleague and I establish an equitable work schedule? Are we going to divide the work into equal units or will one author assume the senior position? How will this judgment determine who is first, second, or third author?

3. If the colleague is senior in rank to me, will he or she perceive his or her role as a boss?

4. How will gender roles affect work assignments? Will male authors expect female authors to take orders and do the typing and secretarial work?

5. Can I trust the coauthor to complete his or her tasks on time?

6. Will ego taint the collaborative process? Is the colleague

flexible or rigid in perceiving how the work should be completed?

7. Does the coauthor pay close attention to detail?

8. Does the coauthor share a similar theoretical perspective?

9. Does the coauthor possess skills that I don't have that are necessary to do the research?

In addition to honestly considering these questions, you may want to give some thought to how your institution will assess your collaborative efforts. While we need to examine more comprehensively how different disciplines reward collaborative projects, the early returns suggest that collaboration confounds the already murky peer-review process (see Ashton-Jones; Broad; Ede and Lunsford; Zuckerman). In the sciences, for instance, where the heavy costs of research often force academicians to work together, it is far more common for an article to be written by five or more faculty members than by a single author. Arnold S. Relman, editor-in-chief of the *New England Journal of Medicine*, has suggested that accountability diminishes when numerous scientists claim authorship (Coughlin). To ensure that all coauthors receive the credit they deserve, Relman has suggested that coauthors "sign a statement attesting to the fact that they actually had a hand in the research and are prepared to take responsibility for it" (Coughlin A6).

If you are going up for tenure or promotion, you may want to take Relman's suggestion a step further and ask your colleagues to write about the nature of their contribution in the by-line to the document. People on the tenure and promotion committee may assume that your contribution to an article was secretarial rather than substantive in nature if you are not listed as first author. Unfortunately, I realize that this suggestion may cause more problems than it is worth. First, colleagues may disagree about the extent and nature of their contributions. Second, requesting that coauthors describe their contributions in a by-line may seem petty because it breaks with tradition. Because this request goes against the giving nature of collaboration, it may even jeopardize future opportunities to collaborate with the same author (or authors).

ANALYZE THE ECONOMIC AND POLITICAL CONSTRAINTS THAT IMPINGE ON HOW YOU WRITE

I once worked with a newly minted Ph.D. in mathematics who enjoyed writing thirty- to forty-page mathematical proofs. Because these extended equations were so difficult to read, this mathematician complained that no one wanted to read his work. He told the members in his scholarly writing workshop that journal editors had difficulty finding anyone willing and qualified to review his submissions. When a colleague in the workshop suggested that he write only ten-page mathematical proofs, the mathematician became upset. "To be really important," he exclaimed, "the proof needs to be long!"

Clearly, you are wise to pursue topics that energize you. Yet if you hope to publish what you write, you must balance your passion with the passions of your audience. Writing thirty-page proofs when even leading experts dislike reading them is like putting your head down and trying to blast through a concrete wall. You may eventually succeed, but the endeavor will knock you silly. Sometimes, as the saying goes, it makes more sense to walk around a wall than to plunge through it.

When you first begin writing scholarly articles, drafting even simple documents may take an inordinate amount of time. With practice, you will soon learn to limit the amount of revising that you need to do. However, if you are a perfectionist, then you may always have trouble completing documents. After all, a piece of writing is seldom perfect. You must limit the amount of time that you invest in each document. Asking the following questions may help you juggle the need to revise with the need to get the work completed and published as soon as possible:

1. Ultimately, how important is the message? Is the material suitable for a first- or second-tier journal or publisher?

2. Given timing and budgetary constraints, is the intended project feasible? Will the cost of the research or conference presentation exceed its ultimate value?

3. Are there any significant methodological problems?

4. Do I have the resources and time necessary to conduct the research?

5. Will this work be respected by the salary-tenure-promotion committee that will evaluate my work?

ANALYZE YOUR SCHEDULE, BREAK THE MANUSCRIPT INTO MANAGEABLE SECTIONS, AND ESTABLISH DUE DATES FOR FIRST, SECOND, AND SUBSEQUENT DRAFTS

As any seasoned professor knows, the academic calendar looks deceptively simple. At solid colleges and universities, where teaching loads rarely extend beyond four courses a year, professors would seem to have large blocks of time to dedicate to their research. Yet experienced professors know too well how time can be absorbed by committee work, by service, by students who need help writing M.A. and Ph.D. theses, and by the demands of course-work. Consequently, you would be wise to set some time aside each day—even if it's as little as thirty minutes—to write, plan, and market scholarly projects. Asking the following questions may help you establish reasonable goals and schedules for completing writing projects:

1. If the document is likely to be a long one, how can I subdivide it into parts that can be written in a realistic schedule?

2. How much time do I have to draft the document?

3. When can I have a second or third draft completed?

4. What reasonable date can I establish for completing this project?

ANALYZE THE RHETORICAL SITUATION FOR THE DOCUMENT

Prior to writing any document, give some thought to your rhetorical situation. In other words, consider what *audience* you are addressing, what *purpose* unifies the document, and what *voice* is most appropriate.

Audience Analysis

When beginning a writing project, you may understandably need to ignore thoughts about audience. Many of us first need to develop the idea so that we understand it before asking how other people will consider it. However, you can save valuable time by identifying your audience and its needs as soon as possible. By answering the following questions, you will be able to determine what information you need to provide and what voice you should establish:

1. Is there really an audience for the idea?
2. What assumptions can I make about my audience's knowledge of the subject matter?
3. Is it possible that the document has multiple audiences? For example, might it be read by graduate students, teachers, scientists, managers?
4. What attitudes about the subject can I presume my audience has? In what ways is my audience biased? Is my audience friendly or hostile?

Purpose Analysis

You cannot know what information to leave in and what to leave out or even how best to organize a document until you know your *dominant purpose* for writing. By asking the following questions *before* you begin to write, you can save time and make your document more effective:

1. What is my primary purpose for writing? Am I attempting to report facts objectively? Am I investigating events? Am I analyzing issues or being persuasive?

2. Do I have competing or conflicting purposes for writing this document? If so, should I write two different documents or one document with distinct parts?

3. What crucial information do I need to shock, educate, or persuade my audience?

Voice Analysis

When attempting to simplify a complex concept, it is easy to overlook the *voice* and *persona* you are projecting. Yet readers are always looking for clues about who you are and how you feel about a subject. Even when you avoid use of the first person and personal references, your readers will be making judgments, rightly or wrongly, about what kind of person you are and about your professional abilities. All aspects of your text give the reader clues about your personality. The words and examples you choose, how you organize your text, and even how you punctuate your sentences affect the tone of your document. For example, no matter how solid your evidence is for a particular claim, you will not be successful if your readers think that you sound sarcastic or condescending. If you don't sound confident, your readers will doubt you. To help establish the appropriate tone for your rhetorical situation before writing, consider the following questions:

1. What inferences do I want my readers to make about me as an author? Do I wish to speak with the voice of a senior scholar, a committed teacher, a benevolent advisor? Do I appear hostile or reasonable? Have I projected a pleading tone?

2. What sort of personas do the writers establish in the periodicals to which I want to submit my work?

FINAL COMMENTS

While time spent prewriting can help prevent extensive revisions, you must avoid the trap of excessive prewriting. The joy of academic writing is often found in the excitement experienced when new ideas shatter plans. Unfortunately, some academicians become so obsessed with prewriting that they never get around to writing and revising. They spend their careers researching ideas in the library, procrastinating because they feel they need to know all about their subject before writing.

To avoid procrastination, you sometimes need to take the plunge and begin drafting. Trust your intuition. After all, you can always come back and do some additional prewriting if you begin to feel unsure about how to proceed. As I will explain in the next chapter, you can sometimes manage your time more effectively by trusting the generative nature of language to guide you toward an audience, purpose, and voice.

NOTE

1. To develop this list of questions, I drew on the essay by Mary Frank Fox and Catherine A. Faver, "The Process of Collaboration in Scholarly Research," on Evelyn Ashton-Jones's essay "Coauthoring for Scholarly Publication: Should You Collaborate?" and on my own experiences as a coauthor.

WORKS CITED

Ashton-Jones, Evelyn. "Coauthoring for Scholarly Publication: Should You Collaborate?" In *Writing and Publishing for Academic Authors*. Ed. Joseph M. Moxley. Lanham, Md.: University Press of America. 269–287.

Broad, William J. "Crisis in Publishing: Credit or Credibility?" *Bioscience* 32 (1982): 645–647.

Coughlin, Ellen. "Concerns about Fraud, Editorial Bias Prompt Scrutiny of Journal Practices." *Chronicle of Higher Education*, 15 February 1989: A4–A7.

Ede, Lisa, and Andrea Lunsford. *Singular Texts/Plural Authors: Perspectives*

on Collaborative Writing. Carbondale: Southern Illinois University
Press, 1990.
Zuckerman, Harriet A. "Patterns of Name Ordering among Authors of Scientific
Papers: A Study of Social Symbolism and Its Ambiguity." *American
Journal of Sociology* 74 (1968): 276–291.

3

How to Draft and Organize
Scholarly Projects

Finding the best way to organize your work is often a dynamic process, one that cannot be simplified into a single formula. Sometimes your plan for organizing a text crystallizes during prewriting, while other times you remain unsure about how to organize your material after writing numerous drafts. And sometimes a document never seems settled or well organized.

Unfortunately, because they were taught by well-meaning English teachers that they should *always* make an outline before writing, some academicians believe that they are violating the rules when they write without an outline. Or, more sadly, when they cannot come up with an outline, some academicians fear that their idea is weak and insignificant, that they lack the critical thinking skills necessary to write well. In fact, recommending that one always outline before writing is based on the foolish assumption that thinking and writing are not related, that first one thinks and then one writes. Also, some people simply abhor outlines, and outlines can be superfluous when the subject being addressed is routine.

Instead of assuming that there is one correct way to organize a document, you may be able to write more successfully if you try a variety of organizing strategies. For instance, rather than always trying to organize your ideas and then writing, you may sometimes need to write a few drafts. If you are troubled by your organization, you can then check the logic of your presentation by outlining what you have just written. In the following discussion, I present six ways to experiment with and shape your ideas:

1. Freewrite drafts.
2. Dictate drafts.
3. Draw a cluster diagram.
4. Draw a pie diagram.
5. Draw an issue tree.
6. Make a formal outline.

FREEWRITE DRAFTS

There seems to be a sort of fatality in my mind leading me to put at first my statement and proposition in a wrong or awkward form. Formerly I used to think about my sentences before writing them down; but for several years I have found that it saves time to scribble in a vile hand whole pages as quickly as I possibly can, contracting half the words; and then correct deliberately. Sentences thus scribbled down are often better ones than I could have written deliberately.

—Charles Darwin

When drafting a significant document, you should not expect yourself to write perfect first drafts unless the matter is very routine. Instead of struggling for the perfect word or phrase and relying on your memory and intellectual skills to rehearse a perfect first draft, you can save time and reduce the agony of getting started by *freewriting*.[1]

Freewriting simply means writing without hesitation. Rather than pausing to reconsider å phrase or looking up the spelling of a word, try to ignore critical thoughts and focus on generating ideas. Although a simple concept, freewriting provides a powerful antidote to an overpowering "internal editor"—the critical, fault-finding self within each of us that says to slow down and wait till the ideas are perfectly formed. As you will find once you have practiced this technique, shutting down the editor within and writing without stopping enables you to (1) develop ideas that you otherwise would not develop, (2) overcome the tightness and frustration associated with beginning new writing projects, and (3) create a flow that helps establish a voice in your prose.

After practicing freewriting for a while, you will find that you can often discover some excellent insights and connections between ideas that more rigid forms of thinking would not have permitted. In addition, freewriting can be a significant time-saving device. In fifteen minutes, you can usually generate as much as 200 to 300 words. Then you can reread the freewrite and attempt to identify the statements worth developing. Eventually you will be able to use substantial chunks from your freewrites as solid drafts requiring little revision.

Freewriting can be an invaluable way to unleash the vigorous voice that characterizes effective prose. When you do a lot of stopping and starting, your prose can sound choppy or forced. When you are summarizing extensive research, the material that you have researched and the order in which you discovered the information can quickly overtake the voice you are attempting to develop. However, when you let your thoughts about the research flow, they often gain a forcefulness, a sense of directness and insight, that they otherwise might lack.

When reviewing your freewrites, identify the details that seem most significant. Put brackets around the sections that you believe are worth keeping. Draw a line through sections that should be deleted. Search for ideas that keep popping up. If they don't seem related to your subject, copy them down on a separate sheet of paper, because they may be surprisingly useful later on. To identify

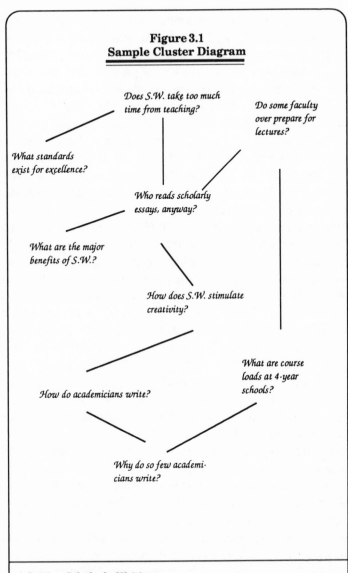

Figure 3.1
Sample Cluster Diagram

Does S.W. take too much
time from teaching?

Do some faculty
over prepare for
lectures?

What standards
exist for excellence?

Who reads scholarly
essays, anyway?

What are the major
benefits of S.W.?

How does S.W. stimulate
creativity?

What are course
loads at 4-year
schools?

How do academicians write?

Why do so few academi-
cians write?

* S. W. = Scholarly Writing
Topic: Why Should We Engage in Scholarly Writing?

the focus that unites the details, summarize in a sentence the substance of the freewrite and then take that sentence, record it on a separate sheet of paper, and use it to begin a second freewrite. By continuing this process of looping from one freewrite to another, you can quickly generate 1,000 words instead of struggling to write 300.

DICTATE DRAFTS

Dictating your ideas and notes can be a surprisingly productive way to begin drafting even complicated essays. By keeping your Dictaphone or tape recorder nearby, you can quickly record insights that occur to you about Project A when you are working on Project C. One obvious advantage of dictating drafts is that you can speak faster than you can write. Also, sometimes dictated drafts have a strong, natural voice. Finally, dictating machines allow you to record insights whenever they occur to you. If you are maneuvering through traffic on your way to work and an idea hits you, you can simply record it then and transcribe the details later.

DRAW A CLUSTER DIAGRAM

When you feel totally disorganized and unsure about your subject, you can draw a cluster diagram. This technique can be useful when you are feeling desperate and totally blocked. Rather than trying to force your ideas into a formal outline, you can pictorially represent them on the page and then draw lines between ideas that seem somewhat related, as illustrated in Figure 3.1.

DRAW A PIE DIAGRAM

When your topic can be separated into discrete categories, you may consider drawing them as a pie diagram (see Figure 3.2). The advantage of a pie diagram is that it allows you to estimate visually how much time you should spend addressing each aspect of your

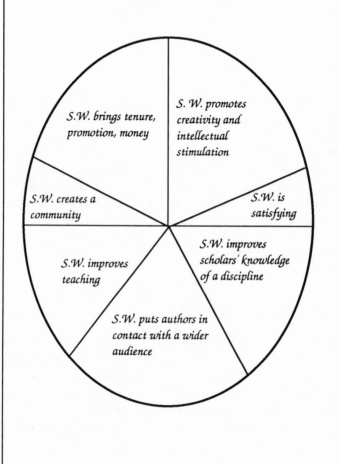

Figure 3.2
Sample Pie Diagram

S.W. brings tenure, promotion, money

S. W. promotes creativity and intellectual stimulation

S.W. creates a community

S.W. is satisfying

S.W. improves teaching

S.W. improves scholars' knowledge of a discipline

S.W. puts authors in contact with a wider audience

* S. W. = Scholarly Writing
Topic: Why Should We Engage in Scholarly Writing?

subject. If you believe, for example, that Issue A deserves a more involved discussion than Issues B through E, you can draw it as a bigger piece of the pie. Of course, when revising a draft, you can redraw the pie diagram to adjust for changes in how you need to develop a project.

DRAW AN ISSUE TREE

When you do have a sense of how events relate to each other and you can put them in a narrative structure or show cause-and-effect relationships, then you can best illustrate these relationships by drawing an issue tree. The primary advantage of an issue tree is that it helps you determine whether ideas are related to each other and the overall theme. As with cluster diagrams, an issue tree allows you to represent your thinking pictorially. However, rather than drawing ideas in a random, disorganized fashion, you can

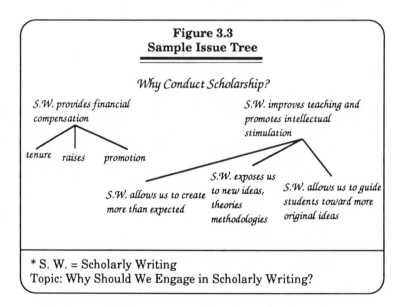

Figure 3.3
Sample Issue Tree

Why Conduct Scholarship?

S.W. provides financial compensation

tenure   raises   promotion

S.W. improves teaching and promotes intellectual stimulation

S.W. allows us to create more than expected

S.W. exposes us to new ideas, theories methodologies

S.W. allows us to guide students toward more original ideas

* S. W. = Scholarly Writing
Topic: Why Should We Engage in Scholarly Writing?

impose order on them, placing them from most general to most specific or vice versa. If you find yourself unable to connect an idea to some part of the diagram, then you will need to reconsider your purpose for writing the document or include the tangential information beneath a more general purpose. For example, the sample issue tree (see Figure 3.3) fails to address several interesting issues that emerged in the cluster diagram: (1) How does scholarly writing affect conceptions of knowledge? (2) How do scholarly writers compose ideas? (3) What use do scholarly writers make of scholarly documents?

MAKE A FORMAL OUTLINE

Writing outlines is probably one of the most frequently mentioned organizational techniques. The advantage of a well-constructed outline is that it will help you identify gaps in your reasoning and presentation.

Figure 3.4
Sample Formal Outline

Purpose Statement: _____
Audience Statement: _____

I. Major Theme Related to Purpose

    A. Subpoint
        1. Example/Explication
        2. Example/Explication
    B. Subpoint
        1. Example/Explication
        2. Example/Explication

II. Major Theme Related to Purpose

FINAL COMMENTS

While freewriting is probably the most powerful drafting strategy discussed in this chapter, you should push yourself to test the other techniques. For instance, once you get over the discomfort of hearing your own voice on tape and once you develop ways to transcribe the most insightful comments, you may find dictating to be an efficient way of overcoming procrastination. If you are a visual learner, then pie, cluster, and issue tree diagrams are far better alternatives to drafting more rigid outlines. As with the other strategies discussed in this book, these drafting and outlining techniques can best be mastered through practice. By working with these strategies over time you will be able to write more focused documents and publish your work.

NOTE

1. The term "freewriting" was coined by Peter Elbow. His innovative book, *Writing Without Teachers* (Oxford University Press, 1973), provides a comprehensive discussion of the benefits of freewriting. I highly recommend this book to all would-be authors who feel blocked and anxious whenever first beginning a new writing project.

4
─────────────────

Guidelines for Developing
a Writing and Research Notebook

While the previous chapters addressed the attitudes and working habits of successful academic authors, this chapter presents a *form* that you can use to practice all of these techniques. If your research writing does not appear note-bound and if you tend to be an organized writer and researcher, then you may want to skip this chapter. But if you are disorganized as a researcher and writer, then you may want to study this chapter assiduously.

Unlike a writer's diary or journal that records daily events in chronological order, a *Writing and Research Notebook* is organized by subject categories. By organizing your ideas and plans in a three-ring binder, you can gather together related ideas, which can help stimulate your thoughts on different ideas. A notebook can help you identify a specific research question, organize your reading notes, draw inferences from what you read, and construct a bibliography. Below are some of the categories that you can use to select, research, refine, and polish scholarly documents. You may want to add some categories to the following ones that more accurately reflect your professional interests.

Table 4.1 Sample Log Sheet			
Date	Minutes Worked	# of Words Written	Goals
1.			
2.			
3.			
4.			
5.			
6.			
7.			

MAINTAIN A LOG

Because you can sometimes feel unproductive even when you are researching sources and methods or doing reading that will lead to writing, you may find it useful to keep a log of the work you have completed and the ideas you have developed (see Table 4.1). The advantage of maintaining a log is that it can help motivate you to work on a project even when you are in a slump and unsure of how to proceed.

MAINTAIN A SCHEDULE OF WRITING GOALS AND RESEARCH DECISIONS

You can use this section to decide which subjects to pursue and to outline the amount of time you will probably need to set aside for prewriting and revising. Because conducting research is typically not a step-by-step process, you will probably want to routinely revise your goals for research, writing, and anticipated due dates. To help develop a realistic schedule, you may find it useful to ask the following questions:

1. How much time can I set aside for finding a topic?

2. When will I have identified the major sources needed to begin writing a solid draft? What sources may be difficult to obtain?

3. When can I develop a tentative description of my rhetorical situation? In other words, when will I have a good idea of the audience, purpose, and voice for the project?

4. Have I thoroughly read the guidelines for authors in the periodical where I would like to publish the manuscript?

5. Will it be possible for me to run my idea by a prospective editor or experienced colleague?

EXPERIMENT WITH FREEWRITING AND SELF-REFLEXIVE WRITING

In this section you can freewrite about any subjects that you choose, and you can also use this section to do *self-reflexive writing*. Essentially this term refers to writing about writing. Psychologists and composition theorists have found that writing about the problems that we are experiencing with different writing projects and writing about specific revising goals can be a powerful way to overcome blocks and improve as writers:

1. What changes can you make in your life that will help you accomplish your writing goals? How can you schedule more time to write?

2. What are your writing rituals? What is the best time of day for you to write? Where do you like to write? (The crowded cafeteria? The quiet study?) How does your writing space influence your writing? Have you ensured that you have the materials on hand necessary to do your rituals?

3. What changes can you make in your environment that will help you achieve your writing goals?

4. What self-talk can you identify that intrudes on your

productivity? For example, does a small voice within you whisper that your ideas lack originality, that the editor and editorial reviewers will dislike your manuscript? Do you tell yourself that you lack the time or ability necessary to get the work done?

5. What kind of social supports can you establish to promote regular writing?

6. What myths about writing and scholarly research do you hold that intrude on regular writing? What changes in *how* you write will help you achieve your writing goals?

7. How is regular writing influencing your attitude about yourself as a writer? Or, if you are having difficulty writing regularly, why do you think this is?

8. How has rejection in the past influenced your perception of yourself as a writer? How has the fear of rejection influenced what you write about?

KEEP A SECTION OF READING NOTES AND THOUGHTFUL EXCERPTS

In this section you can keep a record of the memorable and intriguing quotes that you come across in your reading. If you have read any other guidelines for academic writing, then you probably know that it is commonly recommended that you keep reading notes and bibliographical references on 4-by-6-inch or 5-by-8-inch cards. The great advantage of using cards is that they can be shuffled to help you find the best way to organize your manuscript.

However, if you are short of time, you can make photocopies of the material that you expect to use in your final draft. This will allow you to reread the essays and highlight powerful quotes at your convenience. Of course, to save money, to avoid being overwhelmed by material, and to get you thinking seriously about your subject, you need to be selective about which secondary sources to photocopy.

Figure 4.1
Double-Entry Notebook Form

They [i.e., creative ideas] may indeed occur at times of relaxation, or in fantasy, or at other times when we alternate play with work. But what is entirely clear is that they pertain to those areas in which the person consciously has worked laboriously and with dedication. *Purpose* in the human being is a much more complex phenomenon than what used to be called will power. Purpose involves all levels of experience. We cannot *will* to have insights. We cannot *will* creativity. But we can *will* to give ourselves to the encounter with intensity of dedication and commitment. The deeper aspects of awareness are activated to the extent that the person is committed to the encounter.

—Rollo May, *The Courage to Create*, 46.

I'm absolutely certain that Rollo May is totally right: total involvement in the "encounter" of the creative process is crucial for the emergence of the Eureka moment.

Unfortunately, I think, too many people are too uncomfortable about the intrusion of the disruptive "right brain" or "unconscious." They dislike the creative process because they fear chaos and failure.

How, then, can we encourage people to "submerge" themselves, to lose themselves in an idea or feeling, long enough to experience the Gestalt, the felt sense, the joy, the bliss, the *jouissance?* If people could only experience this passion for the creative process, they would learn that writing is not a boring, mechanical process of filling in completed thoughts in preestablished modes of discourse.

Fi

Place Reading Notes in Double-Entry Form

One very effective technique for avoiding note-bound prose is to respond to powerful quotes in what Ann Berthoff, a writing theorist, calls the *double-entry notebook form.* As you can see from Figure 4.1, you print the direct quote on the left side of the page and then respond to it on the right. There are two advantages to this technique. First, it helps you think about your subject. Second, it helps you step away from your sources and discover your own approach and voice.

Figure 4.2
Writing and Research Goals

Purpose of Project: _____

Audience for Project: _____

Tentative Title: _____

Potential Publishers: _____

Collegial Support: (Should I work on this project with a colleague or by myself? Do I know someone who might have
some interesting information about the subject?)

Tentative Schedule: _____

Prewriting/Drafting Efforts
    Freewriting: _____
    Cluster Diagram: _____
    Pie Diagram: _____
    Issue Tree: _____
    Tentative Outline: _____

KEEP A SECTION FOR NEW WRITING AND RESEARCH IDEAS

The heart of a successful notebook is your record of your best
ideas (see Figure 4.2). Rather than ignoring ideas for new writing
projects that occur when you are in the middle of a different writing
project, you can keep a record of your new ideas in this section.
Your thoughts about your subject are likely to change as you read
more about your subject, discuss your ideas with colleagues,
freewrite ideas about your topic, and write preliminary drafts. Even
if you have a solid idea about what you want to say and how you

want to say it, you should be willing to sabotage this goal if more fruitful ideas come your way and sufficient time remains to develop them. In addition, you may have insights about how you are actually researching or writing your document. For example, while writing a paragraph on page eight of a research study, you may realize that the way you phrased your research question in your journal or report proposal no longer accurately reflects your intentions.

KEEP THE LATEST DRAFT OF YOUR REPORT NEAR YOU SO YOU CAN REVISE WHEN POSSIBLE

Because innovative ideas about your subject and ways to structure it in your report may occur when you are not working on it, you should keep your notebook and the most recent draft of your document with you. Whenever insights occur or you find yourself with some unexpected spare time—for example, when you are waiting in line at the drive-through bank—you can record your insights.

KEEP THOUGHT-PROVOKING ARTICLES HANDY

After maintaining a notebook for a while, it will be bulging at the seams and you will need to remove unimportant material and file it elsewhere. Although you probably will not have space for many outside articles, you may want to keep one or two of the most helpful articles in your notebook so that you can get to them easily when you are looking for inspiration. Ultimately, however, you will probably find it useful to file articles and printed documents in their own three-ring binders or file folders.

MAINTAIN A WORKING BIBLIOGRAPHY

Because you will need to include a bibliography at the end of your document, you should keep careful track of the sources you use while conducting research. It can be quite annoying and frustrating to be forced, after completing your research and writing, to return to the card catalog or periodical shelves to retrieve the information you need to cite your sources properly. This frustration quadruples when you discover that other people have subsequently checked out your materials.

As soon as possible, check to ensure that you understand the form of documentation that you will need to follow. Then be sure to record on your photocopied material all the facts needed in the bibliography—author, title, volume number, publisher, date of publication, and page numbers. Fortunately, most scholarly journals and some commercial magazines print this information on the title page of each article. If not, you had better record it now; otherwise, you may need to retrace your steps.

Of course, as discussed above, if you photocopy all of the materials that you need to write the report and ensure that the reference information is printed on the photocopies, then you can type directly from these materials when constructing your bibliography.

FINAL COMMENTS

Maintaining a writing and research notebook can help you write regularly, set goals, establish priorities, and organize your scholarly endeavors. If you tend to be a disorganized researcher, then the notebook can provide an invaluable focus for creative ideas. Although you can succeed without such a notebook, maintaining one can give you some control over what and how you write.

5

How to Submit and Market Your Work

Whenever possible, you should determine likely avenues of publication for your ideas *before* you write. Rather than assuming that you need to first identify a subject to write about and then do an exhaustive review of the literature, you can manage your time more effectively by keeping a record of the subjects that occur to you when reading professional literature. For instance, what comments have other colleagues made that seem particularly specious? What research do other scholars call for in their implications and conclusions that seems worth developing? Because the impetus to write about a subject often emerges from asking these sorts of questions, you will usually have a pretty good idea about where to submit your work. After all, you can find the most likely publisher for your idea by checking your bibliography and determining which sources you cite most. Once you gain momentum as a scholar, innovative topics will emerge in response to previous writing projects, and your sense of publishing opportunities will be keener as you will be familiar with different journals and editors.

When your first, second, or third choice rejects your manuscript, however, you should not give up hope of publishing it. Remember that reasonable people routinely disagree about what constitutes excellence, and then send the manuscript back out for additional reviews. The information discussed below can help you identify an appropriate publisher, present your work in a professional way, and survive the peer-review process.

FORMAT YOUR WORK IN A PROFESSIONAL MANNER

With today's personal computers and laser printers, there is no excuse for a shoddy presentation of ideas. Your readers—wrongly or not—will judge the quality of your ideas in part by how they are presented. You should, therefore, see that final drafts of all of your documents are carefully formatted. To help your work stand out in a competitive environment, print final drafts on a laser printer. Lasers nearly match the quality achieved by typesetting machines, and they often print eight to ten pages a minute. (Fortunately, lasers have dropped dramatically in price over the last decade. At the educator's price, you can now purchase a solid non-PostScript laser for $800 and a PostScript laser for $2,000.) If you do not have access to a laser, print materials on a good ink-jet printer. Although some of the more expensive ink-jet printers offer a printout nearly comparable to a laser, some users complain that the print of the ink-jets smears. If a laser or ink-jet printer is not available, you should probably print your document on a daisy-wheel letter-quality printer. Although agonizingly slow, the final product of a letter-quality printer is usually far superior to dot-matrix printers that have fewer than twenty-four pins.

Although most publishers want at least one-inch margins on all sides with at least twenty-seven lines per page, some prefer one-and-a-half-inch margins and twenty-five lines per page, so you should check the publisher's guidelines for authors. On the first page of the manuscript, you may want to list your name, address, and phone number. Occasionally editors request a word count.

Figure 5.1
Sample Manuscript Page

George Nelson   222-444-1324
Department of Engineering   Word Count: 2,500 words
University of New City
New City, North Carolina 33617

Structural Analysis of Kaput Bridge

The extent of damage to Kaput Bridge caused by the hurricane that hit Kaput, Florida causes us to re-evaluate its structural integrity.

xxxxxxxxxxxxxxxxxxxxxxxxxxxxxxxxxxxxxxxxxxxxxxxxxxxxxxxxxxx
xxxxxxxxxxxxxxxxxxxxxxxxxxxxxxxxxxxxxxxxxxxxxxxxxxxxxxxxxxx
xxxxxxxxxxxxxxxxxxxxxxxxxxxxxxxxxxxxxxxxxxxxxxxxxxxxxxxxxxx
xxxxxxxxxxxxxxxxxxxxxxxxxxxxxxxxxxxxxxxxxxxxxxxxxxxxxxxxxxx
xxxxxxxxxxxxxxxxxxxxxxxxxxxxxxxxxxxxxxxxxxxxxxxxxxxxxxxxxxx
xxxxxxxxxxxxxxxxxxxxxxxxxxxxxxxxxxxxxxxxxxxxxxxxxxxxxxxxxxx
xxxxxxxxxxxxxxxxxxxxxxxxxxxxxxxxxxxxxxxxxxxxxxxxxxxxxxxxxxx
xxxxxxxxxxxxxxxxxxxxxxxxxxxxxxxxxxxxxxxxxxxxxxxxxxxxxxxxxxx
xxxxxxxxxxxxxxxxxxxxxxxxxxxxxxxxxxxxxxxxxxxxxxxxxxxxxxxxxxx

1

Some guidelines for authors request that authors center the number for the first page about four lines below the last line of text, as illustrated in Figure 5.1. On the top line of each page except the first, you may want to provide a running head, which essentially repeats the first three or so words of your title and gives the page

Figure 5.2
Sample Running Head

"How to Format Documents"   Moxley 2

Begin the text at least four lines below the running head.
> You can indent 5 to 8 spaces for paragraph breaks.
>> Then indent an additional three spaces for block quotes,
>> which are quotes that are more than five lines long that
>> are excerpted from secondary sources.

Remember that there is no one correct way to format texts, yet
you should always be consistent.

---

number. Figure 5.2 shows a standard running head, which you can
adapt to fit your style and situation.

USE VISUALS SELECTIVELY

You can also make your work more visually appealing by using
frequent headings and subheadings. A well-placed illustration or
graph is still worth a thousand words, particularly when your
subject is complicated and presents new information to an audience. Of course, some readers frown on excessive use of visuals,
and a poorly prepared chart can make you look unprofessional,
even somewhat silly. However, a well-placed graph or table can
emphasize and clarify your main points. You know visuals are a
success when readers can quickly summarize the gist of a document by scanning them.

HOW TO MARKET SCHOLARLY ARTICLES

Academic journals are usually produced by nonprofit organizations that are driven by an editor's or institution's desire to develop

and promulgate new knowledge. A *refereed journal* is considered superior to a *nonrefereed journal* because the decision to publish is made by an editor *and* members of an editorial board rather than by a single editor. Because scholars volunteer their time to review manuscripts, you are expected to submit one manuscript to one journal at a time. If you ever do submit an article to more than one journal and you need to retract it from Journal B because Journal A has accepted it, you can bet your year's salary that you will never be published in Journal B. More importantly, word can get around, and you can find yourself unable to publish anywhere. In narrow disciplines where most of the scholars know each other, it is even possible that your manuscript could be sent to the same reviewers by different journals, thereby killing your chances to publish in either journal.

When you submit an article for publication to a refereed journal, editors usually scan the cover letter and manuscript to see whether or not it conforms to the submission standards and editorial mission of the press. Because the better journals and presses are flooded with manuscripts, editors are quick to scrawl their initials on a form rejection letter. Thus a work that you spent years writing may be rejected in ten seconds if you fail to follow the correct form of documentation, fail to submit the required number of copies and a self-addressed stamped envelope (SASE), or fail to present a readable copy.

Some editors of refereed journals take on a *caretaker role* rather than a *leadership role*, sending most submissions out for review and relying strongly on the review process to determine whether or not to publish a manuscript. As anyone knows who has had the unfortunate experience of working with a caretaker editor, one negative review can torpedo your submission even if it is followed by several positive ones. In contrast, more dynamic editors send out only what looks good to them, and they look critically at all evaluations. Most journal editors send a manuscript to *at least* two reviewers. Once the reviews are returned to the editor, he or she will usually synthesize the criticisms and reject, accept, or describe the ways the manuscript can be improved. Caretaker editors will usually reject a manuscript outright if one of the reviews is strongly negative. Even when the editor requests revisions, the manuscript usually will need to pass through the peer-review process again before being accepted.

Because scholarly journals usually do not pay scholars to serve on editorial boards or to review articles, the peer-review process can take a ridiculous amount of time. Since the prestige of a journal is somewhat influenced by who serves on the editorial board and who works as review readers, journal editors are caught in the Catch-22 of asking the busiest scholars to review manuscripts. When a senior scholar is several months late, all the editor can do is write strong letters, complain by phone, or—in the worst case— send the manuscript back out for review to another senior scholar. Some clever journal editors arrange for the top scholars in a discipline to serve on the editorial board but actually send the manuscripts to *review readers*, who generally are active yet junior scholars in the discipline who are willing and able to critique manuscripts quickly.

Once the reviews do come back, they often provide more disagreement than agreement. Before dismissing any critiques as eccentric or petty, however, you should remember that reading is inherently a subjective process. If you hope to reach a broad audience, then you must account for a diverse number of critical responses. This does not mean that you should accept all criticisms at face value. If an editor requests that you resubmit your work after revising it, you do not necessarily need to account for *all* of the reviewers' criticisms. It is possible, after all, that one of the reviewers holds an entirely antagonistic ideological position to yours, and no amount of rewriting in the world will satisfy him or her. When a reviewer seems to be a member of a different academic camp, it is worthwhile calling or writing the editor and asking to have the essay reviewed by a different reader on the next go-around.

If the manuscript is flatly rejected by the journal that you originally targeted it for, you will need to pursue other publishers. To do so, you may want to review the table of contents of the other professional journals to which you subscribe. If an appropriate publisher still has not occurred to you, consult your colleagues, and review *Current Contents*, which reproduces the tables of contents of thousands of scholarly journals. You may also find it useful to scan the sources of information provided at the conclusion of this book. Next, go through a few issues of journals to which you would like to submit your work. By evaluating the current table of contents and editorial policy of a journal, you should be able to determine whether there is a good match between your article and a particular publisher. Record (in your writing and research notebook, if you have one) the editor's name, address, and telephone number and pay particular attention to the editorial policy and submission policy of the journal. Note, for example, whether the journal prefers to publish statistical research, speculative articles, ethnographic research, pedagogical suggestions, or book reviews. What kind of primary audience is the journal targeted for—a trade (that is, a commercial) audience? Teachers? Technicians? Scholars? Scientists? How are the essays written? Do most authors use frequent headings and subheadings, graphs and figures, or lengthy bibliographies and appendixes? Are research methods hidden in appendixes or foregrounded in lengthy introductions? Do most introductions offer hints of the articles' conclusions? Are the manuscripts thick with academic gobbledygook or clearly written? Are most of the authors big names from prestigious institutions? Is it necessary for you to submit camera-ready copy? Are you expected to pay a *subvention*, that is, pay part of the costs of publishing? While asking these sorts of questions is admittedly time-consuming, you can save time now by eliminating unlikely publishers. As much as you might like to publish in Journal X, you really shouldn't bother tying up your manuscript in the peer-review process for three to twelve months if that journal is a long shot.

Because it takes time to research potential publishers, you may want to record your findings now so that you will not need to take the "walk of depression" back to the library to find new places to submit the manuscript after it is rejected. Rank order five or so likely journals for a particular manuscript. When considering the best places to publish your work, consider where the important articles in your field are published, how many subscribers a particular journal has, how often the journal is published, how impressively the journal is formatted, even how impressive the title of the journal will appear to academicians in your department and college who have other specialties.

To overcome the tendency to allow an article to sit moldering in a desk drawer after a rejection, some industrious authors prepare five to ten envelopes for mailing. Thus, when their first choice rejects the manuscript, all they need to do is reprint the form letter, stick the manuscript in the prepared envelope, and send it back out for review.

Should You Write a Query Letter or Call the Editor?

Before writing a cover letter for an article, you should consider calling the journal editor and asking directly whether he or she would be interested in receiving your manuscript. Of course, your goal is not to bully the editor into looking at the manuscript. Instead, if the editor desires, you are willing to submit it provided it gets a quick review. While this human touch probably will not increase your chances of publication, it often will ensure that your manuscript will receive some special attention when it comes in. Moreover, informal contact with editors may result in requests that you write book reviews, articles, or books on related subjects at a later date. Also, if the editor is not interested in your topic, he or she still may know another journal or anthology editor who is looking for material related to your subject.

Even after conducting extensive market research, you may be unsure about whether a particular manuscript is appropriate for a journal. For example, a journal's editorial guidelines could be broad and the scope of the existing table of contents could be quite eclectic. You might also sense that interest in your topic has been exhausted by previous essays in the journal. If you are reluctant to call an editor or if you have heard at conferences or through the academic grapevine that an editor is not particularly approachable, you may want to write a one-page letter describing your project and asking whether he or she wants to see it. Although this task may add a few weeks to the evaluation time for your manuscript, it actually may save you months or even a year. After all, if the journal has a caretaker editor, one who doesn't carefully scan the pounds of manuscripts that come over the transom, then the query letter—since it requires a thoughtful response from the editor—may save your manuscript from unnecessarily entering the peer-review process.

What Do Editors Look For in Query and Cover Letters?

Submitting a poorly written query letter can be compared to driving a nail through your right foot and then trying to run a marathon. If you break with convention in an awkward manner, editors will assume that you are a neophyte. In fact, because so much academic writing is initiated by editors prodding senior scholars, your need to write a query already makes your qualifications suspect. Nevertheless, you can create a favorable first impression by addressing the following points *in a single page* on your institution's letterhead:

1. Demonstrate that you are familiar with the editor and journal. Address the editor by name and relate the current submission, if possible, to earlier works published by the press.
2. Offer a dynamic overview of your project and its significance. Explain how your work contributes to scholarship.
3. Explain your qualifications for doing the work and, if possible, mention other publishing credits.
4. While you certainly want to avoid the impression that you are submitting a rough draft, you may find it useful to express your willingness to make any changes that the editor or editorial board deems necessary.

5. Be sure that you have correctly followed the journal's
   submission requirements. While editors of journals in the
   sciences often do not require a self-addressed stamped
   envelope for the return of the manuscript, most editors of
   journals in the humanities and social sciences will not even
   read your submission if you fail to include an SASE.
   Errors in documentation style are extremely annoying to
   journal editors because they demonstrate your lack of
   awareness of disciplinary standards and typically require
   work on the editor's part to be rectified. From experience,
   editors know that serious errors in documentation are
   nearly always correlated with shoddy scholarship.

Because some journals fail to acknowledge receipt of a manuscript,
you may want to attach a self-addressed postcard so that the editor
can mail it back when the manuscript arrives. This step helps you
avoid the lame excuse that many productive authors have heard at
one time, *"Sorry, we never received your submission. It must have
been lost in the mail!"* If three or four months pass after your
submission has been acknowledged, you would be wise to call the
editor and inquire about it.

HOW TO MARKET SCHOLARLY BOOKS

The process of marketing a book proposal or a book is similar
to, but more rigorous than, that of publishing a scholarly article.
In fact, you can use most of the marketing strategies for journal
articles to help you find a book publisher. There are, however,
some important differences between book and article marketing.

First, while authors of articles typically conduct the research,
write the article, and then send it unsolicited to a journal, many
university press books are actually solicited by editors before any
writing is done. In his survey of fifty-two university presses, Paul
Parsons found that one third of the university press books published each year were acquired by editors before any work was
done. Because of increased competition among university presses,

acquisitions editors are prowling conferences and the halls of academe, encouraging promising junior scholars and pleading with senior scholars to transform important articles into full-length books.

It generally makes sense to determine whether there is any interest in your idea before diving headfirst into the research and writing. To find a publisher for your book idea, you can review the *Literary Market Place*, which provides a list of the major university presses. Take note of the senior editor's and acquisitions editor's name, the number of books produced by each press, and the list-building areas defined by each press. In addition, you may want to consult the annual *Directory of the Association of American University Presses*, available from AAUP, 584 Broadway, New York, NY 10012. Also, examine who publishes the important books in your field and the books that you enjoy reading.

In a three-ring binder make a list of the first dozen publishers you would like to submit your book or book proposal to. If possible, get catalogues of these publishers' books and scan them to make connections between your project and others that the publishers have produced. If one of your colleagues has published a book with a publisher that is appropriate for your project, ask if he or she believes the editor would be willing to speak with you. Perhaps your colleague knows the private phone line to the acquisitions editor or would be willing to call the editor on your behalf. Because of the flood of books that comes over the transom, most editors are unwilling to take phone calls from unknown academic authors.

If your book is already completed, you may feel a strong urge to send twenty or so copies out for review at the best university presses. However, this is a needlessly counterproductive and expensive way to market your work. In his interviews with university press editors, Paul Parsons discovered that many editors dread unsolicited manuscripts and that more and more university presses are unwilling to consider them. In his survey of seventy-four American university presses, Parsons found that only 9 percent of the 9,610 unsolicited manuscripts received by fifty-two presses were actually sent out for review. Ultimately, 2 percent of these 9,610 manuscripts were accepted for publication.

To save time and money and to establish good will with an acquisitions editor, you should write a query letter rather than sending your book. As discussed earlier, query letters need to be energetic and well written. Editors want to know how your book extends the knowledge of your discipline, how it relates to their list, who the primary and secondary audiences are, how long it is, and when it can be completed or if it is already done. Some presses also want a *guarantee of exclusivity*—that is, they want your promise that the manuscript has not been submitted elsewhere and that it will not be submitted elsewhere while being considered by the press. Others want a *right of first refusal*, which usually means that you can submit it elsewhere, but that they have the first right to publish it. If you do submit a book or book proposal to several publishers, you are honor bound to mention this in your cover or query letter.

While submitting a query letter rather than sending the book unsolicited is a more professional approach, it will not guarantee you publication. Parsons found that

> Responding university presses collectively estimated that roughly one of every ten queries results in an editor's request to see the complete manuscript. Of those reaching this intermediate stage, an estimated 18 percent actually proceed through editor review, outside peer evaluation, and editorial committee approval. Overall, then, responding presses collectively estimate that about 2 percent of author queries eventually result in a published book—identical to the percentage of unsolicited manuscripts eventually published. (54)

While practices vary from press to press, book publishers, particularly textbook publishers, tend to send manuscripts out to more reviewers, sometimes as many as seven or nine. Because most university presses pay for the peer reviews, you will generally find that reviewers go into more detail regarding the faults of your proposal or book than they do when critiquing your essays. Unfortunately, reviewers for presses are not necessarily more punctual than those for journals. In addition, academic book publishing adds another curve to the scholarly publishing maze: even if the reviews are mostly positive, your project still may be rejected. For after the review process, the editor needs to win the approval of the press's editorial board. While the role and constituency of editorial committees vary from press to press, they are generally composed of distinguished faculty members from a variety of disciplines at the press's home institution, and their primary role is to ensure that the books published by the press meet scholarly standards (Parsons). Once your project has made it through the review process, however, you are usually assured of publication. For instance, in Paul Parsons's study of fifty-two university presses, he found that "about 3 percent of all manuscripts brought before editorial committees ultimately are denied the imprint" (99).

Before blowing your savings on a wild vacation after hearing that your book proposal has been accepted, you should take a long, hard look at the publishing contract. Even if your book proposal is accepted and you are awarded a small advance, your book can still be rejected once it is completed. Publishers nearly always reserve the right to reject a book that was accepted in proposal form. Because you can always be rejected, acceptance of a book proposal is not necessarily better than no acceptance. After all, in the proposal stage you may sign a lousy contract with a poor publisher. After agreeing to no or few royalties, after signing away copyright on the book, you are honor bound to send the book in to that publisher even if the completed book warrants a significant advance, royalties, and publication with a major press. On the other hand, few scholarly books make much money, so most academic authors are pleased with any book contracts they can get. A good publisher, as the says goes, is the one who signs the contract.

WORKS CITED

Fiske, Donald W., and Louis Fodd. "But the Reviewers Are Making Different Criticisms of My Paper!" *American Psychologist* (May 1990): 591–598.

Parsons, Paul. *Getting Published: The Acquisition Process at University Presses.* Knoxville: University of Tennessee Press, 1989.

Part II

The Conventions of
Academic Discourse

6

How to Write Informative Abstracts

Once you are through researching and writing a report, you may be bored by your subject and eager to submit the manuscript for publication. After working night and day on a project, it is a relief to forget about it for a while. If you have not written an abstract for your report, however, you may have a sudden mood shift, like someone who has slammed a new car into a brick wall after driving it off the showroom floor. Exhausted by your topic, you may feel the urge merely to retype the major transitional phrases and headings in your report and call that the abstract. Though understandable, such an approach is foolhardy. Take this warning from a former fool: act as if you have all of eternity to revise your abstract. Although it is usually the last section written, the abstract is the most important element of many academic documents. Readers frequently scan abstracts to determine whether a document is worth reading.

WHAT IS AN INFORMATIVE ABSTRACT?

Informative abstracts provide readers with an accurate understanding of the gist of a report, including, for example, a statement regarding the significance of the subject, a review of the methodology used and limitations found, important results, discussion of results, and recommendations. Because abstracts are brief, usually less than a page long, they include only the specifics necessary to highlight essential information. Abstracts must be able to stand alone as independent mini-reports because they are often torn from their context—that is, the report proper—and reprinted in computerized databases and printed indexes (such as *Chemical Abstracts*, *Dissertation Abstracts*, etc.). Because of this need to stand independently, you should eliminate references to authorities cited, tables and graphs illustrated in the report, obscure abbreviations, and jargon.

Determining how technical you can be in your abstract is often a tricky proposition. On the one hand, your abstract should present an accurate reflection of the way the report is written. It would be inappropriate, for example, to popularize a report if its subject is inherently technical and if it is aimed at a narrow audience of specialists. Likewise, if the report is written primarily in the passive voice, then the abstract should also be presented in the passive voice. However, you need not slavishly follow the report proper. In the abstract it is acceptable, even preferable, to shake up the organization and give more emphasis to the most significant information.

While you generally want the abstract accurately to reflect the tone of the report, you should remember that even technical audiences enjoy being eased into a complicated topic. Many abstracts fail because the authors have lost perspective of their audience and subject. After spending the majority of their free time researching and writing a study, authors understandably may assume that everyone is familiar with the significance of the subject, with technical terms and abbreviations, and with a methodology. Such assumptions can be quite deadly, however, because they lead to impenetrable prose.

WHY ARE ABSTRACTS IMPORTANT TO READERS?

Abstracts are essential to readers. *Truly essential.* First, readers can scan abstracts to determine whether it is worth their time to read the work. Readers may give the report a careful reading if the abstract seems intelligently composed, if the subject matter seems truly significant, and if the methodology seems solid. In contrast, a reader probably will not read a report if the abstract seems unduly technical, if the focus seems cloudy, if the conclusions are spurious in light of the methodology employed, or if the recommendations appear to exceed the findings.

Second, we understand written information better when a general overview precedes the specifics. Readability experts and cognitive psychologists have found that comprehension of technical material increases when we provide abstracts and introductions that establish the overall context of a subject. In other words, readers appreciate it when we tell them what we are going to tell them, tell them, and then tell them what we've told them.

Third, many computerized databases and printed indexes reprint abstracts so that scholars can keep up with each other's work. Associations and corporations often publish abstracts in given fields and mail them to appropriate scholars and researchers. While a well-written abstract can ensure wide publication, a poorly written one can guarantee anonymity. Thus, if you want to ensure that your work has an impact in your field, then you should work as hard as possible on presenting precise and engaging abstracts.

WHY ARE ABSTRACTS IMPORTANT TO WRITERS?

Because the abstract makes you focus on what is important, you may find it useful to write an abstract for *all* of your academic projects. Writing abstracts can provide a powerful way of reevaluating your logic and of defining purpose. Even if you are not required to present an abstract at the beginning of a report, you will still need to summarize the gist of your document when you write a query letter. Looking over your subject to see what disciplinary assumptions are challenged, questioning the significance of your ideas, emphasizing the important results, addressing limitations in a realistic manner—these activities are essential to helping you separate the wheat from the chaff. In addition, when you work to summarize your report in a sentence or two, you often gain a firmer hold, a tighter perspective, on the nature of your work.

WHEN SHOULD YOU BEGIN WRITING THE ABSTRACT?

Many scholarly authors recommend waiting to write the abstract until the report is completed. While this advice rightly discourages authors from trying to write an abstract before the report is written, it's a bit extreme. The abstract is too important to wait until the last minute. After running a marathon, there's no reason why you have to force yourself to do a forty-yard dash at the finish line. Instead, I strongly recommend drafting the abstract while you write the report.

7

How to Write Effective
Introductions and Conclusions

A successful introduction shares many of the characteristics of a good abstract. Like abstracts, introductions to academic manuscripts often establish a *deductive overview*. Also, introductions generally establish the *context* for the discussion, and they move from what the reader and writer consider *given information* to *new information*. As I mentioned in the discussion on writing abstracts, we can comprehend and recall information better when authors provide an overview of the main points of the document before launching into a detailed analysis of these subissues. Likewise, sentences that explain a text's organization help us comprehend information when we read.

Inexperienced scholars often illustrate their naïveté by belaboring the obvious. Editors of scholarly journals and books, however, cannot allow scholars to take up valuable and expensive space reviewing ideas, research trends, or research methodologies that are printed in detail elsewhere. As a scholarly writer, you may need to write a ten-page introduction to figure out how your work contributes new knowledge. In the polished journal article that emerges from this draft, those ten pages may very well need to be summed up in a single sentence that refers readers to the scholars on whose shoulders you now stand. The only way to determine what common ground you share with your readers is to question their knowledge and interests about the subject. Sometimes you will need to write several drafts before having a firm grasp of the information that is unique and worthy of elaboration.

However, I should mention that occasionally you may not want to provide the customary overview of your purpose or results in the introduction. While you usually will want to clarify the purpose for writing the document in the introduction, you may want to avoid this straightforward approach when your subject matter is likely to be viewed as threatening to your audience. If your ideas are controversial or contentious, then you may first want to establish your credibility by clarifying the ways in which the readers' assumptions are justified. After you have established yourself as a reasonable and knowledgeable scholar, readers may be more likely to reconsider their assumptions.

When your subject matter is quite technical, you can aid comprehension by highlighting how you have organized the document. When revising your introduction, you may want to provide a sentence or two that will offer the reader a sense of how the document is organized. Then in the body of your research you can provide transitional sentences when you move from one aspect of your study to another. You can also use headings and subheadings to limit the number of explicit transitional sentences and paragraphs that are necessary. By the way, if you are not subtle about your transitional sentences, you writing style may be judged as sophomoric by readers. For example, filler phrases like *"The purposes of this research study were a, b, c,"* or *"In the following, I discuss the following issues: a, b, c,"* are so overused, so mechanical and inorganic, that they call attention to your writing instead of your ideas. Thus, if you sense that the reader can follow the flow of your ideas, then don't worry about transitional phrases. Yet balance the need to be subtle with the awareness that transitional sentences help readers understand and recall information. Of course, if your readers are experienced academics, they will require less guidance and fewer transitional phrases.

One trick you may occasionally wish to try is to make explicit references to earlier articles that were published in the periodical that you hope to publish your manuscript in. By saying that Subject A has been hotly debated in the pages of Journal A, you appeal to the editor's ego and desire to shape a coherent discussion on Subject A.

Because scholarly readers are usually a *captive audience*—that is, they need to read your work as part of their scholarly research (as opposed to reading for entertainment)—you may feel less compelled to make your writing interesting. In fact, some scholars focus solely on the technical nature of their work and tend to forget that their readers need some encouragement to continue reading. No matter how highly trained your readers are, however, you can enhance readability and good will by considering how to make your ideas more accessible and entertaining. You are always wise to question if there are any personal anecdotes that you can share with readers that might enliven your writing. If appropriate, you might even consider adding a touch of humor to an otherwise impersonal manuscript.

Finally, as with abstracts, you should not expect yourself to write the final draft of an introduction until the entire manuscript has been completed. This suggestion is often surprising to academicians who were trained by writing teachers unfamiliar with research in composition theory. The notion that you should be able to outline your project and write the introduction before writing contradicts the generative nature of language. Because we learn by writing, the way we shape our work and even what we say often change as we punch our ideas through several drafts. You are wise, therefore, not to expect the impossible at the onset of a scholarly project. If your work is significant and not a routine review of what you already know, then you should expect great difficulty writing your introduction. Remember to trust the thinking process: Your introduction will gain finesse as you work ideas through different drafts. Meanwhile, you may want to consider the following questions to help you get started:

1. In one sentence, what is the purpose of the document?
2. What surprising information is conveyed in the document? Do the results contradict expectations? Did the people that you interviewed say something shocking or highly interesting? Did your survey reveal an unexpected attitude on the part of your respondents?
3. What assumptions does the audience hold about the topic? How knowledgeable are they about the issues that you raise?
4. Would your concluding paragraph make a better introduction than the current introduction?
5. Will the readers feel as if they have been driven off a cliff or have you identified the concluding paragraphs as a conclusion?

HOW TO WRITE EFFECTIVE CONCLUSIONS

Many scholars fail to recognize the importance of conclusions. Even if the introduction forcefully presents the problem and its significance, and even if the body of the document is logical and well developed, you still need to pay considerable attention to the conclusion. After all, these are usually the last words your audience will read. Readability studies have suggested that a powerful conclusion is second only to the introduction in terms of its effect on a reader. Consequently, present the gist of your argument energetically and concisely. If there is a persuasive aspect to your document, this can be an excellent place to present some emotional appeals.

Of course, your rhetorical situation defines how much detail you will need to go into in your conclusion. A 200-page document, for example, will place different demands on you than a conclusion to a short letter. When attempting to draft a memorable conclusion, consider the following questions:

1. What are the broad implications of your work? What recommendations can you make based on the material you have presented?

2. Would it be appropriate for you to speculate on what will happen next?

3. What do you want readers to do once they have reviewed your document? Should they agree with you about the validity of an argument or theory? Should they change their teaching practices? Should they pour their creative energies into examining an innovative research question?

4. Did you pose a question in the introduction that can now be answered? Is there a way of extending a metaphor that was presented in the introduction?

Throughout the time you spend writing a document, you should keep your ear tuned for a clever closing statement. To develop a powerful conclusion, consider the above questions and the most important message you want to leave with your readers. Also study the ways writers you enjoy conclude their documents.

8

How to Shape Effective Paragraphs

Unlike punctuation, which can be subjected to specific rules, no ironclad guidelines can be provided for shaping paragraphs. If you presented a text without paragraphs to a dozen academicians and asked them to break the document into logical sections, chances are that you would get twelve different opinions about the best places to put the paragraph breaks. In part, where paragraphs should be placed is a stylistic choice. Some writers prefer longer paragraphs that compare and contrast several related ideas, while others provide a more linear structure, delineating each subject point by point, paragraph by paragraph.

If your critics have not suggested that you take a hard look at how to organize your ideas, you may wish to skip the following discussion. After all, you wouldn't take breathing lessons unless you had asthma or felt stressed out. Yet, if you are unsure about when you should begin a paragraph or how you should organize final drafts, then you may want to consider the following guidelines.

When you are drafting, trust your intuition about where to place paragraphs. You do not want to interrupt the flow of your thoughts to check on whether you are placing them in logical order. Such self-criticism could interfere with the flow of ideas that is important to being original and establishing a vigorous voice. Before submitting a document for publication, however, it generally makes sense to examine the structure of your paragraphs. Although the following guidelines are not ironclad, they can give you some insights about alternative ways to shape paragraphs.

PARAGRAPHS OFTEN FOLLOW A DEDUCTIVE ORGANIZATION THAT MOVES FROM GIVEN TO NEW INFORMATION

Your goals for the opening sentences of your paragraphs are similar to your goals when writing an introduction to a document: in the beginning of a paragraph, you usually want to clarify its purpose. Most paragraphs in academic discourse move *deductively*—that is, the first or second sentence presents the *topic* or *theme* of the paragraph, and the following sentences illustrate and explicate this theme. Notice, in particular, how Chris Goodrich cues readers to the purpose of his paragraph (and article) in the first sentence of his essay, "Crossover Dreams":

Norman Cantor, New York University history professor and author, most recently of *Inventing the Middle Ages*, created a stir this spring when he wrote a letter to the newsletter of the American Historical Association declaring that "no historian who can write English prose should publish more than two books with a university press—one book for tenure, and one for full professor. After that (or preferably long before) work only in the trade market." Cantor urged his fellow scholars to secure literary agents to represent any work with crossover potential. And he didn't stop there: As if to be sure of offending the entire academic community, Cantor added, "If you are already a full professor, your agent should be much more important to you than the department chair or the dean."
(1)

Notice that it is *not* possible to simply rearrange the sentences in Goodrich's introduction and preserve the same logic. Because the following violates the reader's sense of order, it seems like gibberish:

> As if to be sure of offending the entire academic community, Cantor added, "If you are already a full professor, your agent should be much more important to you than the department chair or the dean." After that (or preferably long before) work only in the trade market." Cantor urged his fellow scholars to secure literary agents to represent any work with crossover potential.

USE AN INDUCTIVE STRUCTURE FOR DRAMATIC CONCLUSIONS OR A VARIED STYLE

While you generally want to move from the *known* to the *new*, from the *thesis* to its *illustration* or *restriction,* you sometimes want to violate this pattern. Educated readers in particular can be bored by texts that always present information in the same way. Note, for example, how Valerie Steele's anecdotal tone and dialogue in the opening sentences to her essay on fashion in academia prepare the reader for her thesis:

> Once, when I was a graduate student at Yale, a history professor asked me about my dissertation. "I'm writing about fashion," I said.
>
> "That's interesting. Italian or German?"
>
> It took me a couple of minutes, as thoughts of Armani flashed through my mind, but finally I realized what he meant. "Not *fascism*," I said. "*Fashion*. As in Paris."
>
> "Oh." There was a long silence, and then, without another word, he turned and walked away.
>
> The F-word still has the power to reduce many academics to embarrassed or indignant silence. Some of those to whom I spoke while preparing this article requested anonymity or even refused to address the subject. (17)

PARAGRAPHS ARE USUALLY UNIFIED BY A SINGLE PURPOSE OR THEME

Regardless of whether it is deductively or inductively structured, readers can generally follow the logic of a discussion better when a paragraph is unified by a single purpose. Paragraphs that lack a central idea and that wander from subject to subject are apt to confuse readers, making them wonder what they should pay attention to and how the different ideas relate to each other.

To ensure that each paragraph is unified by a single idea, Francis Christensen has suggested numbering sentences according to their level of generality, assigning a "1" to the most general sentence, a "2" to the second most general sentence, and so on. Christensen considers the following paragraph, excerpted from J. Bronowski's *The Common Sense of Science*, to be an example of a subordinate pattern because the sentences become increasingly specific as the reader progresses through the paragraph:

1. The process of learning is essential to our lives.

    2. All higher animals seek it deliberately.

        3. They are inquisitive and they experiment.

            4. An experiment is a sort of harmless trial run of some action which we shall have to make in the real world; and this, whether it is made in the laboratory by scientists or by fox-cubs outside their earth.

                5. The scientist experiments and the cub plays; both are learning to correct their errors of judgment in a setting in which errors are not fatal.

                    6. Perhaps this is what gives them both their air of happiness and freedom in these activities. (60)

Christensen is quick to point out that not all paragraphs have a subordinate structure. The following one, taken from Bergen Evans's *Comfortable Words*, is an example of what Christensen considers a coordinate sequence:

1. He [the native speaker] may, of course, speak a form of English that marks him as coming from a rural or an unread group.

2. But if he doesn't mind being so marked, there's no reason why he should change.

3. Samuel Johnson kept a Staffordshire burr in his speech all his life.

3. In Burns's mouth the despised lowland Scots dialect served just as well as the "correct" English spoken by ten million of his southern contemporaries.

3. Lincoln's vocabulary and his way of pronouncing certain words were sneered at by many better educated people at the time, but he seemed to be able to use the English language as effectively as his critics. (63)

EACH PARAGRAPH MUST RELATE LOGICALLY TO THE PREVIOUS PARAGRAPH(S)

Readers expect paragraphs to relate to each other as well as to the overall purpose of a text. Establishing transitional sentences for paragraphs can be one of the most difficult challenges you face as a writer because you need to guide the reader with a light hand. When you are too blatant about your transitions, your readers may feel patronized. To highlight the connections between your ideas, you can provide transitional sentences at the end of each paragraph that look forward to the substance of the next paragraph. Also, you can place the transition at the beginning of the next paragraph, as Valerie Steele does in the following example:

Can a style of dress hurt one's professional career? True to form, most academics deny that it makes any difference whatsoever. But a few stories may indicate otherwise: When a gay male professor was denied tenure at an Ivy League university, some people felt that he was penalized, in part, for his dress. It was "not that he wore multiple earrings" or anything like that, but he did wear "beautiful, expensive, colorful clothes that stood out" on campus. At the design department on one of the campuses of the University of California system, a job applicant appeared for her interview wearing a navy blue suit. The style was perfect for most departments, of course, but in this case she was told—to her face—that she "didn't fit in, she didn't look arty enough."

Another bit of evidence that suggests dress is of career significance for academics is the fact that some universities (such as Harvard) now offer graduate students counseling on how to outfit themselves for job interviews. The tone apparently is patronizing ("You will need to think about an interview suit and a white blouse"), but the advice is perceived as necessary. (20)

When evaluating your transitions from idea to idea, question whether the transitions appear too obtrusive, thereby undercutting your credibility. At best, when unnecessary, readers perceive explicit transitional sentences to be wordy; at worst, they perceive such sentences as insulting (after all, they imply that the readers are too inept to follow the discussion).

VARY THE LENGTH OF PARAGRAPHS TO REFLECT THE COMPLEXITY AND IMPORTANCE OF THE IDEAS EXPRESSED IN THEM

Different ideas, arguments, and chronologies warrant their own paragraph lengths, so the form of your text should emerge in response to your thoughts. To emphasize a transition in your argument or to highlight an important point, you may want to place the critical information in a one- or two-sentence paragraph.

CONSIDER YOUR GENRE AND THE VISUAL IMAGE OF THE PARAGRAPHS

As much as any of the above guidelines, you should consider the genre of your text. Paragraph length is influenced as much by the genre of the discourse as by the ideas being expressed. For instance, newspapers and magazines produced for high-school educated readers tend to require much shorter paragraphs than do academic journals. When evaluating how you have structured your ideas, however, pay attention to whether you have varied the length of your paragraphs. Long chunks of text without paragraph breaks tend to make ideas seem complicated, perhaps even inaccessible to less educated audiences. In turn, short paragraphs tend to create a listlike style, which intrudes on clarity and persuasive appeal. Because long paragraphs tend to make a document more complicated than short paragraphs, you should question how patient and educated your readers are.

FINAL COMMENTS

Paragraphs provide a visual representation of your ideas. When revising your work, evaluate the logic behind how you have organized the paragraphs. Would your presentation appear more logical and persuasive if you rearranged the paragraphs? Next, question the structure of each paragraph. To see if sentences need to be rearranged, determine whether you are organizing information deductively or according to some sense of what is most and least important.

WORKS CITED

Christensen, Frances. *Notes Toward a New Rhetoric*. New York: Harper and Row, 1967.

Goodrich, Chris. "Crossover Dreams: What Academics Need to Know about Agents and the Literary Marketplace." *Lingua Franca* (August 1991): 1, 17–21.

Steele, Valerie. "The F-Word." *Lingua Franca* (April 1991): 17–18, 20.

9

How to Write Book Reviews

Ideally, book reviewers are impartial and qualified scholars. When placed in a prominent journal, a review can guide scholars to theoretical books that redefine a discipline's self-conception and research goals. Reviews can guide teachers, helping them select classroom texts and find useful classroom references. As a final check on the editorial process, reviewers can raise the flag around a book that isn't receiving the credit it deserves, or, if necessary, lower the flag on a weak contribution.

In the world of academic writing, however, book reviews rarely receive the credit or attention they deserve. Given their potential to change the face of scholarship, book reviews play a remarkably insignificant role. In part, book reviews are not treated seriously because the book review process has been tainted by the *Star System*, in which scholars trade off reviews on each other's books. "You rub my back, and I'll rub yours" is the underground code that often controls who reviews what and where it appears. In addition, as Stephen North argued at a recent Conference on College Composition and Communication, editors determine which books are reviewed, an arbitrary decision-making process unparalleled in other academic genres. Also, editors rarely publish multiple reviews of a single book. While authors may struggle for years to compose a useful article, and journal editors usually require extensive revision of manuscripts based on blind reviews, authors of book reviews are often expected to produce the review within a few months. In turn, editors rarely send book reviews out for refereeing, thereby subjecting the process to the will and ideology of the editor. The pressure to publish the review close to the publication date of the book also limits the amount of revision completed.

In addition, the credibility of book reviews is often weakened by who writes them: rather than being composed by senior scholars, many are written by graduate students. Productive senior scholars are simply too busy writing books or consulting to review the works of colleagues or competitors. Now, while we should encourage graduate students to begin contributing to scholarship as soon as possible, we must also question whether they are in the best position to evaluate a book. Without years of reading and writing, can they place the book in the scholarly tradition? Can they truly be expected to critique their mentors? Without the experience of writing or editing a book, will they be unduly harsh in their criticisms? What kind of message about academic writing are they receiving when asked by their mentor-teachers to write a review for one of their books or for a friend's book?

I do not wish to sound unduly negative about reviews, nor do I wish to question the ability of *all* graduate students. Clearly, some highly dedicated graduate students could (and do) run academic circles around us and are capable of writing useful reviews.

You should consider writing a review if you are an avid reader, are capable of writing a balanced review and unlikely to swing toward extremes in your assessments, and are capable of concisely summarizing 400 to 600 pages in 1,200 to 2,500 words. Although book reviews may count as small change in the academic world, the bottom line is that publishing book reviews is much easier than publishing in other academic genres.

FIND A PUBLISHER FOR THE REVIEW

To find a book to review, you can talk with publishers about new releases and study publishers' advertisements for new books. Also, listen to the academic grapevine about who is writing what, and contact an editor of a scholarly journal and describe your desire to write a review. Journal editors routinely sift through the pounds of books they receive from publishers and consult their own lists of potential reviewers or the lists suggested by the publishers.

When querying an editor, describe your credentials, mention any publishing credits, describe your specialty areas, explain why that editor should have that book reviewed, and explain why you have selected it.

DETERMINE WHETHER THE BOOK IS WORTH REVIEWING

Before agreeing to do a review, skim through the book and see whether it is worthy of your time. A poor book is not worth reviewing unless you think it is receiving undue credit. As a general principle, you should try to select books that seem significant to you and members of your community. Just because you have selected an influential book to review does not mean, however, that you should take on the persona of a sales representative. Remember, also, that experienced readers of overly zealous reviews may very well dismiss the review if it appears to be a product of the *Star System.*

QUESTION WHETHER YOU ARE QUALIFIED TO WRITE THE REVIEW

Once you have found a book worth reviewing, take a hard look in the mirror and ask whether you truly are qualified to critique it. Imagine the author of the book and the years of struggle that he or she went through, hoping to contribute meaning. Honestly ask yourself if you know enough about the scholarly conversation to which the book is contributing. Can you place the book in a historical framework? Are you properly familiar with the author's previous works, presuming, of course, that such works exist? Do you know the author, and, if so, is that knowledge likely to intrude on your ability to write a fair review?

AVOID THE IDEAL TEXT SYNDROME

Researchers in composition theory have found that readers usually judge documents by comparing the author's product with what we would have done if we were the writer. Like the horse following the carrot, we often feel frustrated. While we have an image of how the text should be formed, an inchoate sense of excellence, our ability to capture this image in words continually eludes us. Let's face it, we can critique even the most sublime document—note, for example, the endless parade of criticism regarding Shakespeare's work. As reviewers of scholarly books, however, we need to control our propensity to assume that we know the best way to do things. We need to focus on what is really important and describe this information for our readers. And yes, in the spirit of presenting an objective evaluation, we also owe our readers some commentary regarding significant deficiencies. When carefully reading the work, therefore, you may want to divide comments into thirds: One, describe the contents of the book and its organization, while paying particular attention to the new knowledge the book contributes to scholarly discourse. Two, mention the significant weaknesses. Three, focus on the strengths. If you have juggled these three responsibilities, then the author of the review surely cannot fault you, unless, of course, he or she is a relative, in which case you may have a shorter Christmas list.

FINAL COMMENTS

As with all scholarly documents, you would be wise to share what you consider to be a final draft of the review with your colleagues before submitting it for publication. You may want to

ask them whether you have given enough information about the
book for them to understand your assessment of it.

10

How to Write Quantitative Research Reports

You can determine the best way to organize a research report by considering your purpose and by identifying your audience. If, for instance, you are writing for a professional journal in the sciences or social sciences, then your readers would expect you to present the following:

1. an abstract;
2. a statement of the research question, hypothesis, or problem;
3. a review of literature;
4. a review of materials used and methods followed;
5. a results section;
6. a discussion section; and
7. a notes and bibliography section.

In addition to these basic categories, a lengthy study might include a table of contents, a table of figures, and appendixes. Because these sections are inherently logical in descriptions of research, even essays in the humanities and fine arts are likely to use some of these sections to report research findings. Few would dispute that it makes sense to first describe a problem, explain how it was studied, and then report results and implications. Because of different philosophical underpinnings, however, academic disciplines differ in how they organize documents. The methods section that appears in the body of a scientist's report is likely to be relegated to an appendix in a humanist's report or omitted altogether. Some scholarly journals in the humanities expect authors to begin the essay where the scientist ends—that is, with the results section. Argumentative essays and speculative reports are more likely to foreground the importance of a researcher's results and minimize or even exclude discussions of methods. To create diversity and promote reader interest, some authors will use more engaging headings than "results" or "discussion," yet the underlying meaning remains the same.

Because the best way to organize a research report is determined by your audience and prevailing conventions, I cannot offer rigid, absolute rules. To my mind, claims that there is only one way to structure research writing are about as valid as claims that snake oil cures cancer. No one structure can account for diverse audiences and purposes. Instead, you can determine the best way to organize your work by listening to the emerging logic of your prose. Then, when you revise, consider the conventions for structuring ideas that exist for the audience, purpose, and context that you are addressing. With these conditions in mind, therefore, I cautiously present the following conventions as points of departure, not as absolute formulae.

STATE THE RESEARCH QUESTION OR HYPOTHESIS

As discussed in detail in the chapter on introductions and conclusions and the chapter on abstracts, academicians expect authors to provide a brief overview of the research, covering, for example, the significance of the subject, findings, conclusions, and recommendations.

The opening sentences (or paragraphs, depending on the length of the manuscript) of your investigation should identify your research question, methods, and essential conclusions. Don't be concerned about repeating information expressed in the abstract. Although you are wise to avoid redundancy whenever possible, academicians expect some repetition from the abstract to the introduction. Also, don't worry about giving away your best conclusions early.

REVIEW THE LITERATURE

After briefly clarifying your purpose, findings, and methods, you may wish to present a separate section that reviews the scholarship related to your topic. However, in most scholarly and professional writing, lengthy discussions of the literature are taboo. Academicians expect scholars to ground observations and interpretations in available literature throughout the document and not just in a section in the introduction. Yet they are quickly bored by serious discussions of what they already take for granted, so you will want to explain succinctly how your ideas or findings refute existing assumptions or previous studies.

REVIEW MATERIALS USED AND
METHODS FOLLOWED

Particular disciplines have very specific rules about how to conduct research. To be taken seriously, your research must conform to these methodological conventions. In the sciences and social sciences, authors are usually expected to describe the materials and methods used to conduct the research. Whether you expect others to repeat your study, if you fail to provide the details needed to reproduce it, your work will lack credibility (and publishers). In fact, one of the central tasks of reviewers is to evaluate whether the methodology is reproducible.

If you are using a well-known and accepted method, then a few references to the major studies that have employed this method should suffice. On the other hand, if you are adapting someone else's methods or using a controversial approach, you will need to defend the methodology, explaining why you have chosen it and how it provides an accurate measure of the problem being investigated. You can usually increase your chances of publishing your work by following established methods of inquiry. One of the main problems with using unorthodox approaches is that they require you to substantiate them, thereby diverting attention from what matters: your results.

Because a flawed research design is one of the most common reasons for rejecting a study for publication, ask experienced researchers to look over your plan *before* you conduct the research. Only after several of your colleagues have agreed that your method seems logical and feasible should you proceed.

While conducting the research, you will find it useful to keep a written record of the materials used. Cite generic or chemical names rather than trade names. Remember, be precise in the amount and kind of materials used so that your readers can follow exactly in your footsteps. If your investigation involved selecting subjects, describe the means used to select them.

When you survey people, provide a copy of the questionnaire either in the body of the report or as an appendix. Most academicians want to know how you developed the survey, whom you submitted it to, how many people responded to it, and, as much as possible, the characteristics of the sample who responded to the survey and how closely these characteristics match those of the targeted population (for example, their sex, age, address, years of experience, etc.).

Descriptions of how you conducted an interview are often unnecessary and can even be counterproductive. However, you still may wish to elaborate on the setting in which you conducted the interview and on the specific questions that you asked.

After working night and day on a project, it is quite easy to forget to include some details because they seem obvious. As a result, once the study is completed, ask a qualified peer if the methods section includes all the information necessary to conduct the research. Here are some standard questions that reviewers and editors ask when critiquing research studies:

1. Is the method traditional and accepted? Did the author cite the appropriate authorities who have used the method?

2. If the method is unusual, did the author provide sufficient evidence to warrant its application? Was sufficient credit given to the originators of the method?

3. Did the author use the best possible methodology to study the research question?

4. Was the method used correctly?

5. Finally, did the author provide sufficient details so that the study can be replicated? Has the author explained *what, how, how much,* and *when*?

PRESENT RESULTS

The heart of a successful research report, of course, is the results. After quickly scanning an abstract or introduction, many readers will skip ahead to the results and discussion. In fact, many readers will only study the method section if they doubt the results. Academicians are curious about how your results refute or support earlier studies that explored a similar research question and employed a similar methodology (if, of course, such scholarship is available). In some disciplines, such as the sciences, authors are expected to separate the results from a broader discussion of their implications. In contrast, scholars in the humanities expect authors to interweave their results with a discussion or argument.

Most research studies generate more data than need to be reported. On some issues you may have gone fishing and come up empty, while other issues that may have appeared tangential to your primary theme may prove significant and require emphasis. Academic honesty need not translate into going into monotonous detail about all of your results, yet if some results appear to contradict major patterns in the data, you cannot ignore them. When seeking a thesis that explains the data, question whether any common *themes* or major *points of disagreement* can be found in the data. Did you find what you set out to find? This rigorous process of finding patterns in the data can involve throwing out large chunks of information that simply are not helpful or important. It may take days—even months—of analyzing and organizing the data for you to determine major trends and how best to express them.

Because illustrations are expensive to produce, the notion that a picture is worth a thousand words is still true in academic writing. If you can succinctly present results in a statistical table or graph, you should consider doing so. Because illustrations cost more to produce, however, use them sparingly and only to report significant results. Academic publishers cannot waste space and money just to pepper your text with impressive looking tables. Also, remember that it is not necessary to explain your results in prose if you have captured them in a table or graph, yet you should mention their presence in the text. Consider the following additional questions when evaluating your tables and figures:

1. Have you labelled the axes of tables and graphs? Will your readers understand the abbreviations used?

2. Is an illustration truly necessary? Are the results already apparent in the text?

DISCUSS RESULTS

At last, it's showtime. Now you can interpret the theoretical and pedagogical implications of your results, clarifying how the study adds to and contradicts the work of previous scholars. Here you can tackle the tricky questions and unresolved issues highlighted by your results. You can proudly point your finger into the scholarly territory that needs exploration.

After the tedium of earlier sections of your report and the pressure to produce significant results, you may feel impelled to wax philosophical on the implications of your study. Indeed, many scholars rightly fear that insignificant results will warrant rejection of a manuscript. Unless the matter is highly controversial, a study that merely confirms earlier research lacks the winning punch of a study that breaks new ground. While these are realistic concerns, you need to balance the urge to reveal eternal truths with the need to analyze your data critically. Few editors or readers will accept a giant leap from your results to profound conclusions. In the long run, claiming that you have discovered cold fusion may bring more despair than accolades.

PROVIDE ACKNOWLEDGMENTS, NOTES, AND BIBLIOGRAPHY

In the concluding section of your report, you can acknowledge your indebtedness to friends and colleagues who helped you complete the report. If accepted by the journal you are submitting your work to, footnotes that elaborate on tangential issues may be included. Finally, you should acknowledge indebtedness to all of the scholars you have quoted or paraphrased in the report. (See Chapter 15 for a more complete discussion of documenting sources.)

11

How to Write Qualitative Research Reports and Literary Nonfiction

> Objectivity is passé. Few academics now believe that they can achieve objectivity—or that this view from everywhere-and-nowhere is even a desirable goal. Everyone seems to agree that we can never write anything except from a situated and interested point of view.
>
> —Peter Elbow

Many academics have grown weary of the institutionalized passive voice, of excessive jargon, of the rigid structure of traditional research reports. Even the role of the objective scientist has been questioned as we have come to understand that knowledge is socially determined and shaped by personal desire. Academicians in many disciplines are challenging the positivistic assumption that truth exists as an independent entity that can be measured and quantified. Because they conceive meaning to be context-dependent, some academicians no longer believe that we can generalize from a sample to a larger population. Numerous disciplines, such as psychology, sociology, anthropology, history, religious studies, and education, are developing new ways to plumb the depths of human behavior that do not fit comfortably into the positivistic, scientific paradigm.

Although many academics disagree about the appropriate way to conduct qualitative studies such as ethnographies, case studies, and focus groups, most would agree that these alternative forms of research place greater demands on the author than do traditional forms of research. Because disagreement about what qualitative reports should look like is so widespread, authors of such works are less firmly guided by convention than when following a more traditional methodology. Even within specific disciplines, qualitative studies differ because scholars disagree about the value and practices of qualitative research. Unlike the quantitative researchers, they cannot assume that their work should be segmented into five major sections: introduction, methods, results, discussion, and conclusions. Scholars across the disciplines cannot agree on whether ethnographers or case-study researchers can generalize from a small sample to a larger population. Many qualitative researchers now reject this impulse toward generalization as contrary to the primary goals of qualitative research—that is, to understand specific communities and people. Qualitative researchers cannot even agree about how active a role an ethnographer should play in the community being studied. While some ethnographers formally interview respondents and tell them that they are researchers, others work incognito.

Authors of *literary nonfiction* are in a quandary similar to that faced by qualitative researchers: no rigid conventions exist for how to shape speculative or persuasive essays or other nonfiction documents that employ traditional fiction techniques. Frankly, those of us interested in language and style have tended to focus on novelists rather than nonfiction writers. As a result, attempts to classify the defining attributes of qualitative studies and literary nonfiction must be viewed skeptically. Nevertheless, by noting the work of some master stylists, I can at least touch on a few of the features that these genres share: (1) they are driven by a strong persona, passion, and a speculative tone, and (2) they employ some of the stylistic devices used by novelists, dramatists, and short story writers. The following excerpts from distinguished writers illustrate how we can make our writing more elegant by incorporating these features. Naturally, I assume that all of the standards for writing well, as reviewed throughout this book, can help us achieve this goal. Yet I argue in this chapter that successful writers go a step beyond ensuring that their work is readable: they engage our interest by surprising us, by violating our expectations.

WHY NOT SHARE YOUR PASSION AND SELF?

Much academic writing appears anemic and drab because authors cloak their passion for the subject in excessive jargon and passive constructions. I do not mean to suggest that all quantitative researchers are guilty of adopting a pedantic, detached tone. In fact, some of the greatest scientists have shared their passion and excitement in traditional academic genres as well as in essays for broad audiences. For example, when discussing the coral formations at the Keeling Islands in a professional periodical, Charles Darwin wrote, "It is remarkable how little attention has been paid to encircling barrier-reefs; yet they are truly wonderful structures" (225). And in these brief excerpts from his popular account of how he and Francis Crick discovered the DNA code, James Watson reveals his passion and excitement for scientific discovery:

> Despite the messy backbone, my pulse began to race. If this was DNA, I should create a bombshell by announcing its discovery. (147)
>
> . . .
>
> As the clock went past midnight I was becoming more and more pleased. There had been far too many days when Francis and I worried that the DNA structure might turn out to be superficially very dull, suggesting nothing about either its replication or its function in controlling cell biochemistry. But now, to my delight and amazement, the answer was turning out to be profoundly interesting. (148)
>
> . . .

> After lunch I was not anxious to return to work, for I was afraid that in trying to fit the keto forms into some new scheme I would run into a stone wall and have to face the fact that no regular hydrogen-bonding scheme was compatible with the X-ray evidence. As long as I remained outside gazing at the crocuses, hope could be maintained that some pretty base arrangement would fall out. (150)

While some empirical scientists have had the courage to share their passion and involvement with their subject, even a cursory look at academic periodicals shows this to be the exception rather than the rule. However, it is undoubtedly true that the newer qualitative forms of research and the growing popularity of literary nonfiction offer contemporary writers a chance to share their passion and involvement with their subject matter. Perhaps because they believe that the persona of a detached experimenter does not make the research any more objective, or because they believe that all research is subjective, authors of qualitative studies and literary nonfiction often have strong, opinionated voices. After reading their essays and books, you may feel that you know them.

In some ways the following excerpt from Patricia Adler's ethnography *Wheeling and Dealing* follows a rather traditional organizational structure in that it clarifies the context for her investigation of a subculture of California "wheelers and dealers," and also presents the theory that emerged from her research. Although academicians trained in the sciences and social sciences might initially be put off by her use of the first person, I think it offers an important alternative to the drab, institutionalized passive voice:

> This is [a] study of a community of drug dealers and smugglers and the social scene they inhabit. These operators constitute the drug world's upper echelons, as they import and distribute tons of marijuana and dozens of kilos of cocaine at a time. In part, the extremely illegal nature of their trafficking activities makes these individuals cluster together for both

business and social relations, forming a deviant subculture which reflects common norms and values. This subculture provides guidelines for their dealing and smuggling, outlining members' rules, roles, and reputations. Their social life is deviant as well, as evidenced by their abundant drug consumption, extravagant spending, uninhibited sexual mores, and focus on immediate gratification. They are the jet-setters of the drug world, living the fast life, pursuing the whim of the moment. . . .

The methods I used to study this group were direct and personal. With my husband as a research partner, I spent six years in the field (from 1974 to 1980) engaged in daily participant observation with members of this dealing and smuggling community. Although I did not deal, myself, I participated in many of their activities, partying with them, attending social gatherings, traveling with them, and watching them plan and execute their business activities. I thus came to know members of this subculture, and formed close friendships with several of them. In addition to observing and conversing casually with these dealers and smugglers, I conducted in-depth, taped interviews, and cross-checked my observations and their accounts against further sources of data whenever possible. After leaving the field, I continued to conduct follow-up interviews during periodic visits to the community until 1983. (1)

In the field of composition and rhetoric, Ann Berthoff has often provided a strong, controversial voice. As a sample of how she whispers gossip in your ear and yet makes you rethink an age-old myth—that writing can't be taught—note how Berthoff uses a single bit of dialogue to capture a popular misconception in academia, that writing theory lacks intellectual rigor:

A friend of mine who has for some time devoted his intellectual energies to teaching himself and his young colleagues to teach writing and who recognizes the political imperative to draw out the practical implications of theory was warned not long ago by a colleague who noticed that instead of his literature seminar my friend was offering one on rhetorical theory and composition pedagogy: "Stay away from that stuff! It'll rot your brain!" This man, a distinguished critic and litterateur, had not earned the right to make that judgment, having retreated to the defensive position so attractive to cynics and the lazy, as well as to despairing men of good will, viz., *nobody can teach anybody to write*. (279)

When drafting documents, try to be flexible about the voice that your work should take. At first you might even want to write in the first person because this voice can help you establish a natural rhythm and develop original ideas. You can always eliminate first-person references when they seem inappropriate in light of your audience.

TRY INCORPORATING SOME OF THE STYLISTIC DEVICES USED BY NOVELISTS, DRAMATISTS, AND SHORT STORY WRITERS

Instead of asserting, "This is what X means," fiction writers allow characters to speak about X, and then they expect readers to think, "Oh, so this is what X means." In turn, qualitative researchers and authors of literary nonfiction essays often borrow the narrative voice of the fiction writer. For example, rather than telling readers what they think, some nonfiction authors will offer proverbs and dialogue to show what they think and why.

Ethnographic and case-study approaches to studying human behavior and social organizations often read more like novels or short stories than like academic essays or scholarly monographs. Ethnographers often depict the people that they are studying in a realistic way and expect readers to draw their own conclusions about the ways in which the subjects' environment shapes behavior. Rather than bundling up the results of research into a concise paragraph near the introduction, an ethnographer may wish to tell the story of the community—to *show* what he or she witnessed—so that readers can draw their own inferences about the values of the community. The example below, taken from Douglas Harper's ethnographic study of the lives of tramps, is an excellent example of how an ethnographer can provide samples of conversations between members of the community to illustrate their values rather than explicating them in a traditional academic voice:

I was drinking beer with some tramps one night in the fall of 1973. Jack and Eddie had buddied up when Jack picked Eddie "out of the gutter" in Wenatchee, and he'd taken him along to a job he'd arranged picking apples. Jack had an old car and called himself a rubber tramp. Eddie didn't say much and he didn't work very hard. He looked old and worn out but Jack had an interest in him for some reason and was always saying things like: "Now Eddie, you aren't going off to drink that old wine no more, now are you?" And Eddie would shake his head back and forth—he wasn't going back; he wasn't going back.

I didn't know how they'd ended up together, but I thought that they must have known each other someplace down the road. Jack was talking about the times he'd had: jobs, cars, drunks, bad rides, when Eddie interrupted: "Last job I had was making brooms for fourteen cents an hour—made two-hundred-forty dollars in sixteen months."

Jack banged his beer down on the table and stared at the other tramp: "Two-hundred-forty in sixteen months?"

The tramp looked like he'd wished he'd kept his mouth shut. He finally nodded and started telling us about twenty years behind the bars of San Quentin, Alcatraz, and other prisons I'd never heard of. Jack kept looking at him like he couldn't believe his ears, and I was a little surprised the subject hadn't come up in the month they'd been together. Jack finally asked him what he'd done to get himself in so much trouble and [the] tramp said: "It's checks—always little chicken-shit checks. My problem is my education—I know

how to write my name. Did you ever think of it? Just sign
your name and they give you money. It never fails to amaze
me to find out my name's still good after all the trouble I've
been in." (1)

Now, with the exception of the formal use of the colon rather than
the comma to introduce dialogue, this introduction to Harper's
superb ethnography on tramp life reads more like a novel than a
sociological study. It isn't until the final chapter, in fact, that
Harper introduces the more scholarly tone and apparatus that
academic readers are accustomed to, such as references to secondary sources and heavy interpretation.

In addition to *showing rather than telling*, authors of speculative
pieces tend to use extensive metaphors and images. In part these
images and metaphors are used to make the work more lively, but
they are also used to make readers think. In the following excerpt,
the King of Metaphors, John Gardner, explains that he learned to
revise prose by coauthoring a textbook with Lennis Dunlap, *The
Forms of Fiction*:

Night after night for two full years we would work for five,
six, seven hours on what sometimes added up to three or four
sentences. He drove me crazy, and he wasn't so kind to
himself, either: often we had to stop because the stress of
working with a young man as impatient as I was would give
Lennis a histamine headache. *Gradually I came to feel as
unwilling as he was to let a sentence stand if the meaning was
not as unambiguously visible as a grizzly bear in a brightly
lit kitchen.* I discovered what every good writer knows, that
getting down one's exact meaning helps one to discover what
one means. (18–19, italics added)

It isn't every day that a grizzly bear interrupts breakfast. As usual,
Gardner has selected a provocative image that emphasizes the
importance of his message: every sentence must stand alone, firm
and precise.

Some images are used to convey passion and anger. When the audience is not sympathetic to the author's message, such attempts may seem overly manipulative and ineffective. For instance, in *ProfScam: Professors and the Demise of Higher Education*, Charles Sykes titles one of his chapters "The Crucifixion of Teaching," and throughout his book he uses venomous metaphors and images to turn readers against professors and academic scholarship. At one point, for example, he says that professors care as much about how teaching assistants teach as they do about "a soccer match in Bulgaria" (69). He also suggests that professors are raping their students: "The rape of classroom teaching in the universities takes several forms" (61). Before using such emotionally charged metaphors and images, question whether they are fair and accurate; otherwise, you run the risk of alienating rather than persuading your audience.

Some authors manage to use images in a playful yet provocative way. For instance, when assessing what methodological approaches writing teachers use to decide how and what to teach, Stephen North suggests that teachers—particularly those who have not conducted research—often rely on *lore* to decide what to do. To describe how lore is passed from teacher to teacher and how it controls how we teach, North suggests that lore is like a house inherited by writing teachers:

The House of Lore, as it were: a rambling, to my mind delightful old manse, wing branching off from wing, addition tacked to addition, in all sorts of materials—brick, wood, canvas, sheet metal, cardboard—with turrets and gables, minarets and spires, spiral staircases, rope ladders, pitons, dungeons, secret passageways—all seemingly random, yet all connected. Each generation of Practitioners inherits this pile from the one before, is ushered around some of what there is, and then, in its turn, adds on its own touches. Naturally, the structure is huge, sprawling. There are, after all, no provisions for tearing any of it down. Various portions of it can and almost certainly will be "forgotten" and "rediscov-

ered" again and again. A wing abandoned by one generation
will be resettled (and maybe refurbished) by another. And
note, too, that there is nothing to rule out parallel discovery
or re-invention, either; so the House of Lore has many rooms
that look very much alike. (27)

Scientists and others interested in the creative process have noted
that metaphors can control how and what we think and what we
believe is possible. If we believe that our world is controlled by
the Trinity, for instance, then like Kepler we will seek to reconcile
physical properties and mathematical relationships with our assumptions about God the Father, the Son, and Holy Spirit. After
providing a comprehensive review of the use of metaphor in
science and drawing on the work of Max Black, Jerome Bump
concludes: "Metaphorical models are in fact indispensable tools
for the generation of creative hypotheses and effective explana-
tions in science. . . . Metaphors enable us to make new connections
and see things in a new way" (447).

FINAL COMMENTS

When it comes to defining excellence in literary nonfiction and
qualitative reports, we have more questions than answers. We need
to take a close look at the works of leaders in our disciplines to
determine what makes a text credible and persuasive.

Meanwhile, however, we can agree that the element of *surprise*
may be the most compelling feature of literary nonfiction and some
qualitative studies. In part, academic authors can surprise readers
by breaking with conventions. As discussed above, for instance,
we can surprise readers by sharing our passion for a subject and
by using figurative language.

WORKS CITED

Adler, Patricia. *Wheeling and Dealing*. New York: Columbia University Press, 1985.

Berthoff, Ann E. "Rhetoric and Hermeneutic." *College Composition and Communication* 42 (October 1991): 279–287.

Bump, Jerome. "Metaphor, Creativity, and Technical Writing." *College Composition and Communication* 36 (December 1985): 444–453.

Darwin, Charles. "Keeling Islands: Coral Formations." In *Writing about Science*. 2nd ed. Ed. Elizabeth C. Bowen and Beverly R. Schneller. New York: Oxford University Press, 1991. 222–238.

Gardner, John. *On Becoming a Novelist*. New York: Harper and Row, 1983.

Harper, Douglas. *Good Company*. Chicago: University of Chicago Press, 1982.

North, Stephen M. *The Making of Knowledge in Composition: Portrait of an Emerging Field*. Portsmouth, N.H.: Boynton/Cook, 1987.

Sykes, Charles J. *ProfScam: Professors and the Demise of Higher Education*. Washington, D.C.: Regnery Gateway, 1988.

Watson, James. "Finding the Secret of Life." In *Writing about Science*. 2nd ed. Ed. Elizabeth C. Bowen and Beverly R. Schneller. New York: Oxford University Press, 1991. 140–152.

12

How to Compile an Anthology of Original Essays

If you are patient, eager to organize ideas and files, and prepared to prod senior scholars into doing their best work, then you should consider conceiving and editing an anthology of original essays. Editing anthologies can be an enjoyable way of working with other people to produce original ideas rather than working alone. You can get to know on a first-hand basis some of the leaders in your field, which ultimately may help you publish articles and books and find funding for grant proposals. Getting in touch with the *invisible college* can be an exhilarating way of escaping the doldrums of working with lackluster colleagues and departments trapped in nineteenth-century methods and ideologies.

Before starting an anthology, however, you should know that some academicians are misinformed about the difficulty of this task. Many assume that editing journals and anthologies is not particularly difficult. Conceiving, compiling, and organizing anthologies of original essays does not earn the respect it deserves in academia. Like the overweight, beer-guzzling armchair quarterback critiquing world-renowned athletes on a weekend football game on TV, some armchair academicians are blinded by their ignorance and jealousy. Just as the armchair quarterback doesn't know what happened on the practice field on the Friday before the game, the armchair scholar isn't aware of the extensive letter writing, editing, and revising that is involved in compiling a successful anthology. As you will see from the following discussion, organizing an anthology can be more difficult than writing an original treatment on the same subject, yet the benefits can be worth the effort.

To begin, you need an original idea. By reading the scholarship in your discipline, you can define a dozen or so questions that are troubling and interesting to the members of your community. What fundamental questions do the senior scholars keep posing at the end of their journal articles and books? You may also consider organizing a *fetschrift*, that is, a collection of articles elaborating and extending the contributions of one of the major theorists in your field.

Once you have identified a topic that attracts excitement, you can begin the arduous task of getting other scholars excited about your idea. The secret to compiling a memorable anthology is to involve the senior scholars in your discipline. This is not the time to pay back your friends—at least not all of them. Instead, ask yourself what theorists you have enjoyed reading since graduate school. Whom do you admire most in your field? Who is writing on topics related to the subject that you have identified? This latter question is particularly crucial. You probably won't be able to motivate senior scholars to write for you on a subject tangential to their interests. After all, you can only offer them a few copies of the anthology, a moment in the academic limelight, so you are essentially imposing on their good will. The leaders in your field do not need to work for you. Editors are already clamoring for their manuscripts. The only real way you can attract them to write for you is to give them an opportunity to write about a subject that they care deeply about.

Getting the top people is crucial if you hope to generate excitement about the book. *Also, scholar stars are often stars because they write well.* These endowed chairs and productive scholars know what the anthology article should look like; they know how to document their sources; they know how to urge journal editors to have your book reviewed; they won't back out at the last minute (unless you present a shabby product). These dynamic thinkers have earned their readerships. While you may want to fill a hole in your treatment and provide space for a friend, you may find that some junior scholars write essays requiring excessive revision on your part. Editing a friend's twenty-five-page essay down into a twelve-page essay can result in exactly what you had hoped to avoid: friction in an otherwise smooth relationship and lost time. Thus, let me warn you here: don't offer slots to academicians who cannot write or who do not understand the editorial process. Avoid weak egos who do not understand the importance of revision.

Once you have a list of a dozen or so senior scholars in mind, you need to contact them. You should not call them on the phone or write them and say, "Hey, I'm organizing an anthology and I thought you'd like to contribute an essay. You can decide on a topic, decide where you'd like me to place it in the anthology, determine the documentation style, and set a deadline." Instead, you need to play an aggressive role in the conceptualization and editing of the book. You need to decide the major questions posed by your theme and even come up with tentative, engaging titles that would challenge and interest the contributing scholars.

First, however, you are wise to solicit a commitment from a few well-known senior scholars in your field. Your book will be stronger and more publishable if you can attract major theorists or researchers. Review current essays and see which scholars everyone quotes in their introductions. Then you need to find out who among your friends or colleagues knows these scholars.

At the same time, you need to work at polishing the proposal you will eventually submit to the authors and the prospective publisher. In a few pages, the proposal must define the book's purpose and intended audience. You need to compare your proposed book to books currently available and show how your book extends the scholarship on a particular subject. You will need a tentative table of contents, and a list of scholars and short by-lines for each scholar, that is, 40- to 100-word reviews of their scholarly credentials. (See Chapter 13 for a more complete discussion of the form of book proposals.)

In our scenario, however, your proposal is still quite rough, and you do not have a list of contributing scholars or even a complete idea of contents. Nevertheless, you do have an overview of the topic and its significance, so you can use this information to write some letters to the senior scholars. In a concise way, let them know about your idea, and in a paragraph or so explain your credentials for editing the book. Until you attract a few senior scholars, you are like a shipwrecked, dehydrated sailor in a lifeboat who is lost at sea. Yet if your idea is a good one, scholars will surface like submarines all around you.

Once you have attracted two or three major scholars, you can pick up the phone and do some networking. Contact the authors you wrote to earlier and let them know who has agreed to contribute. Contact the new scholars that have been recommended by your committed scholars. In a few months, you may have a dozen or so scholars and you will have entered *the invisible college*.

The invisible college can be a heady, invigorating place. If your department is composed of inactive scholars or professors who find other methods more appropriate and other subjects more interesting, you may be inspired by getting in contact with scholars at other colleges and universities who are fascinated by the issues that drive your scholarship. Also, you will probably find that your list of scholars has changed dramatically since you first composed it based on an overview of the literature of the subject. Members of the invisible college know each other; they share drafts of manuscripts and invigorate each other by collaborating on topics and sharing ideas. Each year they gather at the important conferences and share ideas and references about special graduate students. More important to you at this juncture, however, they also share phone numbers of other scholars who would be likely to contribute to your book. Also, because they have a stake in its development, they will often suggest that you call a friend of theirs at a particular publisher. Based on one important idea, you now have a new group of colleagues to work with, and you may even have a short list of contributors in mind.

Because you still may not have a publisher, you do not want to ask your colleagues to write their chapters yet. Instead, all you want is a 250-word abstract clarifying their contribution to the book as a whole. Also, as mentioned earlier, you need a brief summation of their qualifications.

When shaping your list of contributors, you should examine the male-to-female ratio. Editorial committees are becoming increasingly sensitive to the need for gender-balanced books. Also, you should attempt to get as national a distribution as possible. Unless you are focusing on a local issue, one that your university press might pick up, you need to find scholars beyond your institution.

If you have engaged the interest of senior scholars, then you probably will have little trouble attracting a publisher. However, as discussed in Chapter 13, acceptance of a book proposal does not guarantee publication. If your people write boring essays that you cannot improve, you will be out in the cold. Fortunately, if you have attracted truly solid scholars, they will write sizzling chapters. In any case, because of their experience, they know the score and will not bother you over the next two years about when and if the book will be published.

After receiving an acceptance letter from the publisher, you need to share the good news with your contributors: We're on! Our topic—your idea—will make a superb chapter! Let's get to work!

At this point, you move from pleading scholar to the boss. You must clarify the length of the chapters; share with your contributors any concerns addressed by the publisher's readers and editorial board about their proposed chapters; define the form of documentation to be used; establish how long excerpts can be before copyright permissions are required; give details about heading styles and whether figures and tables are desired; ask that chapters be submitted electronically; and set a firm deadline. Now comes the rub, however. Because you have attracted senior scholars, you will find that they are busy and unable to meet your deadline. Of course, you need to give them a reasonable amount of time—say six months—to write the essay. However, if my experience is indicative of the process as a whole, it will probably take at least a year for first drafts of all of the essays to come in. Professors, like everyone else, tend to procrastinate, and if you have selected productive scholars, they are probably juggling numerous other projects.

When the essays do come in, you may be in the unfortunate position of needing to critique and revise chapters written by people you were weaned on in graduate school. This is heady stuff. Let me warn you again: proceed with caution. First, remember that subjective factors cloud our evaluations of manuscripts. I can honestly admit, for example, that a few chapters in books that I edited seemed weak and yet were earmarked by editorial reviewers as particularly exemplary. If you are troubled by an author's chapter, you may find it helpful to ask knowledgeable colleagues to look it over and let you know what they think of it. If the author has presented junk, you cannot accept it, nor would it be wise to write a long letter that elaborates on *all* of the weaknesses and errors found in the text. Instead, call the author and ask for a few important revisions. Chances are that the author will make all of the necessary changes on the next go-around. If the piece comes back weak or patched together, you will need to reject it from further consideration.

One trick to ensure that you get the best work possible from your authors is to share with them a few of the best chapters from other contributors. Also, share your proposal and introduction to the book with the contributors so that they can see how their contribution fits into the book as a whole. To help develop cohesion in the book, encourage authors to discuss each other's contributions. Write polished letters to your authors and share published materials related to their topic from time to time to show that this is a professional endeavor and that you are committed to helping them develop the best possible chapter. Once you are satisfied with an author's chapter, you can accept it for publication, pending final approval of the publisher's editorial committee.

If you are in the unhappy position of needing to get a manuscript desktop ready, then you may want to translate the authors' chapter files into your word processing program or have them retyped.[1] Once you have copy-edited and typeset the chapters, you should send the proofs back to the authors for final proofreading. No matter how carefully you have edited the manuscript, mistakes are likely to rear their ugly heads with additional rereading. Also, some authors still need to make minor changes before being totally satisfied, and since you want them to give you their best effort, it makes sense to be flexible in this regard. Finally, if you give the authors a second look at their manuscripts, they cannot be too angry at you if the published version still has a few errors.

If all this sounds like a lot of work to you, you're right. In fact, organizing an anthology of original essays can be much more time-consuming than simply sitting down and writing the book yourself. The advantages of this genre, however, are many: you transcend the petty rivalries of your department, enter the invisible college, and meet interesting and productive scholars. Once you have proven yourself, these people can help you get tenure, promotion, and jobs at other colleges and universities. With so many serious scholars working together to address a single subject, your chances of producing a memorable book are quite high. Finally, a well-orchestrated anthology can be more marketable than a single-authored university press book because the scholars who have contributed to the book have a stake in helping market it. If you enjoy working with talented people and are especially well organized, then you should consider editing a scholarly monograph.

NOTE

1. If you are preparing the anthology with the use of an Apple Macintosh computer, then you can use Data Link Plus Transfer to translate documents written on IBM computers. This sophisticated translation program can provide perfect translations of numerous different word processing programs.

13

How to Write Book Proposals

Rather than dedicating several years of your life to writing a nonfiction book that is unpublishable, you should first write and submit a polished book proposal. While you may be unable to entice a publisher into signing a contract based on a proposal, you can at least get a preliminary sense of whether your idea is marketable. Also, if the publisher sends your proposal out to reviewers and then shares the reviewers' criticisms with you, you can use this information to help develop a more useful book. Finally, if the publisher does offer you a contract, you can write with the peace of mind of knowing that the concept is viable and the book publishable. However, as I will explore in more detail below, a signed contract does not guarantee that your project will be published. Most publishers include an *acceptability condition* that allows them to back out of a publishing contract if a manuscript receives poor reviews.

Of course, you still might want to write a book that does not win a contract in proposal form: publishers can be wrong, and they do change their minds. Yet, if you are attempting to earn tenure or promotion, be cautious and try to put your energies into projects that can earn contracts or at least garner interest before being written. Once you have tenure, then you can settle down and do the serious work that is more chancy.

Even if you have already completed a book, you may still want to submit a book proposal rather than the entire book. This may seem like an odd way of doing things, yet there are several reasons for such an approach. First, agents and editors are extremely busy, and they usually can make a decision on whether a book is viable by reading a first chapter or proposal. Second, it is possible that a publisher might reject your book, take some good ideas from it, and then share these ideas with authors already under contract with the publisher. According to W. Ross Winterowd, textbook authors sometimes face this problem.

WHAT SHOULD THE PROPOSAL LOOK LIKE?

Editors expect nonfiction book proposals to explain the book's purpose and market, the features that will distinguish the book from its competition, the expected contents, the date it will be published, and the author's (or authors') qualifications.

What Is the Market for the Book?

No matter how well you write or how original your ideas are, your book needs a market. Publishers want to see that your text fits into a particular niche. Thus, you should let the publisher know if a required course would use your book, what its likely enrollment is, and who generally teaches it—graduate students, adjunct faculty, or junior faculty. Incidentally, because of the highly specialized nature of most academic work, publishers are wary of promises that a book will be adopted in numerous courses. Although enthusiasm can be infectious, be careful about offering the moon.

What's the Competition?

Your goal in this section is to show how your book synthesizes all of the positive features of the competition. You also want to emphasize the unique features that will make your book stand out from the crowd. By writing in an informed way about the market for the book, you will illustrate that you are capable and prepared to do the work. Conversely, suggesting that your book is designed to compete with books that have lost money and earned a poor reputation will quickly earn you a form rejection letter.

Textbook editors are fond of the phrase *evolution, not revolution* because they want books that preserve the necessary conventions yet contribute in new ways to a discipline. Thus, your proposed contents need to be roughly similar to those of leading books in the field, yet somewhat different; your substitutions and deletions must reflect how your discipline is evolving. When critiquing your proposal, editors and reviewers will want to see that you are aware of the leading books that your proposed text will compete with. You can determine the best sellers and competition by examining books that have gone into multiple editions. Read reviews of books hot off the press. Talk with sales representatives to find out which books are doing well and why, and which ones are failing.

Present a Tentative Table of Contents

Your critics will expect some changes in the proposed contents and organization once you start writing the book. In fact, your critics may view this change as one of the major ways in which they can contribute to your book's development. However, at the proposal stage you are expected to provide a brief abstract for each chapter, clarifying the focus and perhaps offering a sample of likely headings and subheadings.

Present a Condensed Curriculum Vitae

Book publishers do not want to be bothered with lengthy academic curriculum vitaes (CVs). They do not need to know every committee you have served on and whose theses you have directed, nor do they need a comprehensive list of all of your publications. Instead, you should sift through your CV and determine what past activities and publications qualify you to write the proposed book. Most publishers would be pleased to see a one- or two-page review summarizing pertinent publications, listing your academic degrees, and mentioning where you earned them. It generally makes sense to include any teaching awards you have won. Finally, mention your academic rank and whether you are tenured. (Because they know that nontenured faculty are under pressure to publish research articles, and because most salary-tenure-promotion committees do not view textbooks as original contributions, textbook publishers prefer to offer contracts to tenured faculty.)

Enclose Some Sample Chapters

Unless you have an extensive publishing record or your subject is especially hot, you will probably need to submit at least one sample chapter along with the proposal. Just to see if your topic is marketable, however, you may want to shop a proposal around without sample chapters. Before offering a contract and an advance, most publishers want to see several sample chapters to get a better feeling for the book and to evaluate your writing style. It generally makes sense to enclose the introductory chapter and a chapter that is unique. Prior to receiving a contract, you may feel reluctant to pour your energies into writing sample book chapters. However, you should avoid submitting rough drafts to publishers, because they might assume that the draft represents your best effort. Once publishers reject a book idea, they usually do not want to see it again, even if the chapters are in more final form.

A NOTE ABOUT TEXTBOOK PUBLISHING

Understandably, many academicians are attracted by the big bucks of commercial textbook publishing. Indeed, if you could write a handful of texts that capture a fair share of the market, you could retire on a yacht in the Bahamas. For instance, if you wrote an introductory text that sold 40,000 copies at a wholesale price of $40 per book and your contract called for a 15 percent royalty on the first 20,000 copies and 18 percent on the remaining copies, you would make $264,000 on the first year's sales. Next, while noting that over 10 million students enroll in college courses each year, imagine writing a best seller, one read by 1 million students, and you can see why publishers receive thousands of textbook proposals each year. Before going out and buying a new car or a new home, however, you should take a hard look at the decision-making process that editors follow before agreeing to publish a book.

The Audience Problem

Many textbook authors to whom I have spoken over the years have expressed great frustration over the audience problem. While an author may write a text that students would love, it still must pass muster with the book's primary audience: the instructors. The audience problem may be the major reason why many textbooks are so bland. Like politicians who fear alienating their electorate, authors can weaken their presentation by trying to be all things to all teachers.

When evaluating your proposal and your textbook, be sure you are not undercutting the authority of the instructors who will be using your book. Ridiculing traditional pedagogies that you abhor makes as much sense as tailgating and beeping your horn at a cop for driving too slowly.

Textbooks and the Greasy Brass Ring

So far I have highlighted the advantages of textbook publishing. Yet, like the expensive Corvette that is composed mostly of plastic, we should not be fooled by the song and dance of a fast-talking aquisitions editor. The phrase "many are called but few are chosen" is particularly true when it comes to being a successful textbook author.

The competition begins at the proposal stage. According to Paul Smith, the senior editor of the College Division at D. C. Heath, "thousands of proposals [are] submitted to publishers in a given year, . . . only about one in forty-five is accepted, and only about half of these survive the rigors of authoring, development, and production processes to become actual, published textbooks" (160). Even after a manuscript has passed through the proposal stage, through numerous revisions called for by dozens of critics, it is not assured success in the marketplace. In fact, Smith warns that most published texts do not prove to be successful:

> In my experience, approximately one-third of all new titles published in a given year fail, costing publishers money and effort and authors unremunerated loss of valuable time and energy. Another third of the new titles published will eventually make some money (perhaps only what it cost to produce them) and remain in print for at least three years or so, but often their sales are so slow (even if steady) as to not warrant a revision. The last third will become profitable, some exceedingly so, and be revised regularly to maintain a steady share of their respective markets. (160)

If your aim is to fatten your bank account, you might be wise to play the lottery rather than invest four to six years of your life in writing a textbook that ultimately may fail. If, however, you hope to help your students and to make a difference in a subject you care deeply about, then keep reading so that you can know about the dangers ahead.

Four years? Six years? Dangers ahead?

Yes, it takes at least four years for quality textbooks to reach print. First, writing innovative texts is not a simple matter. They require closer attention to detail than sophisticated journal articles, since they are longer and are reviewed more rigorously. Also, no matter how quickly the author writes his or her draft, the review process can take a lifetime. Textbook publishers rely extensively on the reviews of experts in the discipline to evaluate the potential contribution of a manuscript. In addition, by sending a text out to ten or twenty different scholars over the life of the book's development (while paying a nominal $100 to $250 reading fee), the publisher can generate enthusiasm and commitment to the book, ultimately leading to adoptions.

What To Look Out For in the Contract

Experienced textbook authors invariably assert, in one way or another, that "the textbook author who represents himself or herself in contract negotiations has a fool for a lawyer" (Winterowd 151). In his critique of publisher-author relationships, W. Ross Winterowd encourages textbook authors *always* to reject the first offer, to assume that other publishers would be interested in your proposal, and to be willing to step away from the negotiating table. Although he acknowledges that they are standard boilerplate, Winterowd encourages authors to negotiate contracts that have an *acceptability condition* and an *assignment condition.*

Essentially, the acceptability condition means that the publisher can reject the manuscript at any point—even the night before the manuscript is scheduled to be printed. According to some contracts, the publisher does not even need to notify the author about the reasons for rejection. Because editors often move from house to house, and because publishing companies are being bought out by international conglomerates that tend to overlook any *unwritten contracts* between author and editor, Winterowd contends that textbook authors cannot accept the editor's word that the author will be permitted to revise his or her work:

The acceptability condition in contracts should be so framed that publishers (1) have a time limit of, say, two months in which to inform authors of acceptability or unacceptability of the manuscripts; (2) must supply authors with a specific list of the particular reasons for the manuscripts' unacceptability;

(3) must give authors a reasonable period in which to revise
the manuscripts in accordance with the list of particulars.
(148)

In turn, Winterowd warns that the problem with the assignment
condition is that the publishing company can sell your contract to
another publisher, who in turn can sell your contract to another
publisher, and so on. With each sale, your manuscript could be
held up with new editors, who might not view your manuscript as
one of their priorities. Your manuscript would also have to pass
through additional nitpicking critics, resulting in even more revisions. Also, your book could die in committee if the publishers felt
that it would compete unduly with some other book on their list.
Consequently, Winterowd wisely suggests that your contract be
revised to include the following statement: "The contract cannot
be assigned by either party without the written consent of both
parties" (149).

With salary-tenure-promotion committees frowning on textbooks and with the odds against financial compensation, authoring
textbooks may not be a wise choice, particularly if you do not yet
have tenure. Then again, textbooks allow you to shape your
discipline and teach vast numbers of students. Writing textbooks
can also improve your teaching while still allowing you to fulfill
your scholarly obligations. If successful, you can know that you
have helped shape your discipline, that perhaps your words might
help some promising students find their professions. If you love
writing and can simplify complex material, then you should consider writing a textbook.

WORKS CITED

Smith, Paul A. "The Art and Agendas of Writing a Successful Textbook
    Proposal." In *Writing and Publishing for Academic Authors*. Ed. Jo-
    seph M. Moxley. Lanham, Md.: University Press of America, 1992.
    159–180.
Winterowd, W. Ross. "Composition Textbooks: Publisher-Author Relationships."
    College Composition and Communication 40 (May 1989): 139–151.

14

How to Write Proposals
for Grants

Proposal writing is not all that dissimilar to more traditional forms of academic writing. To be successful, proposals must be audience-sensitive, informative, and concise. Like traditional research reports, proposals typically describe a problem, outline its significance, present methods to study or solve the problem, and outline ways to evaluate the success of the proposed plan.

Unlike scholarly essays, however, funded proposals can pay your salary, fund business travel and office expenses, and have your dean knocking on your door to take you out to lunch. Another advantage is that with a few minor revisions you can send one grant proposal to a dozen different foundations and, if you are lucky, accept funding from all of them.

RESEARCH POSSIBLE FUNDING AGENCIES

With more than 24,000 foundations to choose from and with $10 billion up for grabs, chances are that your interests will dovetail with those of a few foundations. You can probably develop some excellent ideas for grants by reading the guidelines for submitting to these foundations. To determine the best foundations to shoot for, you should check with your institution's development office. Judith Ruderman, a prolific grant writer, encourages scholars to get to know development office personnel: "You would be wise to begin your search for money by learning to navigate the resources of your own campus. Once you and your interests become known to these personnel, they will often direct appropriate notices of funding opportunities to your attention" (182).

To develop a sense of grants available, you should also review the books published by the Foundation Center (79 Fifth Ave., New York, N.Y. 10003, 1-800-424-9836). For example, *The Foundation Directory* offers information on "the nation's largest, most influential foundations—those that hold at least $1 million in assets or give at least $100,000 in grants each year" (The Foundation Center 2). In addition, *The Foundation Directory Part 2* reviews "the next largest set of foundations—those with grant programs between $25,000–$100,000 (The Foundation Center 2). To develop a firm sense of audience, you may also want to consult *Foundation 1,000* (formerly *Source Book Profiles*). This reference book explains "which foundations to target in your subject area; whom to contact; what the current program interests are; which nonprofits have already received grants for similar projects and who the officers and staff are (The Foundation Center 4).

When researching possible foundations, you will want to examine what proposals have been funded in the past, how much money was usually awarded, and what application materials are available. Find out whether your institution has received funding from any of the prospective foundations and try to speak with colleagues at your institution and other institutions who submitted winning grant proposals to the prospective sponsor.

Once you have a few prospects in mind, you can run your idea by your institution's development office personnel. Most universities and colleges require the development office to approve all proposals before they are submitted for review to ensure that competing proposals are not sent to the same foundation and that the proposals fall within the institution's priorities. Also, foundation personnel tend to be experts in marketing and proposal writing, so you would be wise to draw on their expertise.

After studying a foundation's proposal guidelines, researching the composition of its board members, and studying its funding history, you may want to call the foundation's program officer to determine if any hidden agendas are lurking in dark corners. Proceed with caution because some foundations view such calls negatively. The benefits generally outweigh the risks: an informal chat with a program officer can be invaluable. You may learn, for example, that board members dislike qualitative research methods or that a project similar to yours has already been funded at a different institution. You may also want to ask the funding officer about grants that have been funded in the past. If possible, try to get a copy of a few of these grant proposals.

Finally, some experts suggest contacting trustees for prospective foundations. Perhaps this is an acceptable tactic if you are a friend of the trustee or know a friend of a friend. Although this tampering with the decision-making process can and does work, its professionalism is questionable.

UNDERSTAND THAT DECISIONS ABOUT WHOM TO FUND ARE ALWAYS SUBJECTIVE AND OFTEN POLITICAL

Experts in grantsmanship often encourage would-be grant writers to first volunteer their services as evaluators for proposals. One advantage of being a reader for the National Science Foundation, the National Endowment for the Humanities, or a similar big-name foundation is that you will see how other bright people write proposals that win funding. Another is that this experience will make your name known within the inner circle. Ideally, proposals are based on their scientific and artistic merit, yet, given the subjective nature of interpretation, it is understandable that knowledge of the author can cloud the judgment of the critics. (This is particularly true when you are competing for on-campus funds.)

Also, by being a part of the game, you might get an early start at a new grant cycle on a subject that is new for the agency.

STUDY THE PROPOSAL GUIDELINES AND EVALUATIVE CRITERIA

Little is as important as meticulous examination of the criteria the reviewers will use to judge your proposals. If the funding source aims to help pregnant teenage girls, then you had better be sure that your grant will result in helping this population. If the guidelines call for a one-page description of need for the proposal, then you should not write two pages.

EXAMINE YOUR AUDIENCE AND VOICE

The success of many proposals hinges on the author's sense of audience. As always, you need to consider the audience's level of interest and knowledge about your subject. Most grants require you to pay extra attention to this concern. As an author of a scholarly article, you are typically writing as insider-expert to other insiders. In contrast, when writing a grant, you are usually writing as an insider-expert to people who are outsiders and definitely not experts in your field. Thus, you must avoid jargon and simplify your presentation and content.

You may have the greatest difficulty simplifying complex issues without shortchanging them. To determine whether you have successfully simplified your presentation without sacrificing too much accuracy, you may want to pass copies around to experts and nonexperts and ask them the following questions:

1. Can you summarize what I have said?
2. Have I grabbed your interest? What changes can you suggest to make the document more appealing to the foundation readers?

3. Have I established the importance of the project?

4. Do I appear credible, enthusiastic?

5. Does my project seem feasible? Will the methods allow me to achieve the goals?

WRITE AN ACCURATE BUDGET SECTION

If you assume that you will receive less than you request, you may feel the urge to overestimate your expenses. The problem with this approach is that it can give the critics a sense that you will play fast and loose with the foundation's money. Instead, you should be meticulous in your analysis of how the money will be spent. As shrewd business people, trustees of foundations and their personnel often want to get the biggest bang for the buck—that is, they want to help as many people as possible, dollar for dollar.

BRING OUT THE BIG GUNS

When determining where to award grants, foundations are understandably concerned with the track record of the proposal writer and that of the writer's institution. Given their concern that the work be completed as promised, foundations are usually more inclined to fund an author who has published extensively on a subject or who works for a prestigious institution.

You should not give up hope if you work for a relatively obscure institution or if your publishing record is sparse. First, some foundations have special programs to help junior faculty. Second, you may be eligible for some local funding that national scholars cannot touch. Third, you can bring out the big guns—that is, you can solicit letters of support from well-known scholars who work for prestigious institutions. Naturally, gathering support letters can take considerable leg work, and you will need to get started long before the due date for the proposal.

LEARN FROM YOUR MISTAKES

The competition for grants is so fierce that you should not blame yourself if your proposal is rejected, nor should you simply throw it into a bottom drawer. Instead, set your anger and frustration aside and call or write the program officer. Ask what the reviewers disliked about your proposal and what suggestions they offered for improving it. Ask for copies of proposals that were funded. You can then use this information to determine what revisions are needed and if you should resubmit to this source, or if you should submit the proposal elsewhere. As with the more traditional academic genres, diligence is the successful grant writer's key to success.

WORKS CITED

Foundation Center. "Fundraising and Nonprofit Development Publications and
        Services." New York: Foundation Center, 1992.
Ruderman, Judith. "How to Find a Find and Catch a Catch: Writing the Winning
        Grant Proposal." In *Writing and Publishing for Academic Authors*. Ed.
        Joseph M. Moxley. Lanham, Md.: University Press of America, 1992.
        181–204.

15

How to Document Sources, Observe Copyright, and Provide Acknowledgments

Many academicians would rather discuss where to buy a cemetery plot than discuss how to cite secondary sources. In comparison to the inherently interesting nature of the creative process, the nuts and bolts of documenting sources seem insignificant and tedious. Yet the careers of some mighty academicians have crashed and burned because they failed to pay attention to the intricacies of source documentation and copyright law. As a result, I discuss in this chapter how to avoid plagiarism, how to copyright manuscripts, how to arrange for permissions, and how to provide appropriate acknowledgments.

HOW TO DOCUMENT SOURCES

Unfortunately, each discipline has its own standards for how to cite material. While interdisciplinary work would be much simpler if scholars could agree on one or two major citation systems, presently dozens of citation systems are endorsed by various professional organizations. For example, English teachers and scholars involved in composition and rhetoric follow the guidelines prescribed by the Modern Language Association (MLA). In turn, psychologists and others in the social sciences follow those established by the American Psychological Association (APA). The bible for editors of scholarly journals and university presses is *The Chicago Manual of Style*. Biologists use *The Council of Biology Editors Style Manual*. Many lawyers use Harvard Law Review's *A Uniform System of Citation*. Chemists follow *The American Chemical Society's Handbook for Authors*. And engineers have numerous style formats to choose from, such as the Engineers' Joint Council's *Recommended Practice for Style of References in Engineering Publications*, the American Society for Mechanical Engineering *MS-4: An ASME Paper*, or the American Institute of Industrial Engineers' *The Complete Guide for Writing Technical Articles*. Regardless of the details about where periods, commas, and parentheses should be placed, all citation systems have one goal in mind: to ensure that authors acknowledge the work of other scholars whom they have cited or been significantly influenced by. In addition, citation systems enable scholars to review bibliographies and thereby become thoroughly informed about a subject.

If you write in a discipline that publishes journals requiring different forms of documentation, you may want to inquire among your peers whether a software program is available that can automatically translate documentation styles. For example, *WP Citation* allows users of WordPerfect 5.1 to generate bibliographies in over 400 publishing styles, such as Chicago, MLA, or Turabian. (This program is available from Oberon Resources, 147 East Oakland Avenue, Columbus, Ohio 43201-1208, 1-800-243-3833.)

Because disciplines have different guidelines for listing author, place, and date of publication, these matters will not be reviewed in detail here. Instead, I discuss below the conventions for documenting sources that transcend disciplinary boundaries. In particular, I encourage you to avoid excessive quoting, to ensure that you do not mistakenly quote a secondary source when paraphrasing, to introduce the context and credibility of references, and to *power quote* to establish a persuasive persona.

AVOID EXCESSIVE QUOTING

Academicians do not want to read miscellaneous quotes thrown together helter-skelter. Documents that rely extensively on quotes tend to lack voice or authority. If you place quotes after every few lines, your ideas and voice take second stage to other people's ideas and voices, which contradicts your reason for writing—to share your thoughts. Although no firm guideline can be prescribed, stylists often suggest limiting direct quotes to 10 percent of the total length of your document.

You will, however, occasionally find it useful to quote directly. For example, you might want to provide a direct quote if the material goes to the heart of your discussion or argument; if it is so well written that it cannot be condensed further; if it contains an eyewitness account of an event; or if it is written by a prestigious scholar whose comments are crucial to your purpose.

ENSURE THAT PARAPHRASED SECTIONS ARE ACCURATE AND PROPERLY CITED

When you paraphrase another scholar's original ideas, you must acknowledge your indebtedness. This does not mean, however, that you should cite everything you read. Instead, you need to determine whether a particular insight is considered *given information* by other scholars in the field. In other words, if many scholars are expressing similar ideas or insights, then you may be able to consider this information to be *public domain information*. When in doubt about whether an insight is unique to a particular scholar, however, you should cite the scholar.

Also, when reviewing your paraphrased passages, check to ensure that you have not repeated any phrases from the secondary source without putting quotation marks around them. If you have read an article many times by another scholar, you can easily repeat

Figure 15.1
Sample Draft & Critical Reading Questions

Gilligan investigates women's moral development, concluding that women "make different sense of their experience, based on their knowledge of human relationships" (172). Furthermore, Gilligan asserts that "a recognition of the differences in women's experiences and understanding expands our views of maturity and points to the contextual nature of developmental truths" (174). Women, as connected knowers, prefer to find their voices "through open-ended, exploratory, often autobiographical writing in which [they] assume a sympathetic audience (Lamb 11).

As skilled critical readers, academicians would probably ask *"Who is Gilligan? What methods did Gilligan use to investigate women's moral development?"*

Here they might ask "How so?" and "What does this mean?"

Here critical readers might wonder what cultures Lamb studied before reaching such a profound generalization.

Belenky et al. describe five epistemological positions that characterize women's ways of knowing. Based upon interviews with women only, their research offers an alternative perspective to William Perry's epistemological positions derived from male students at Harvard.

How did Belenky et al. derive "five epistemological positions" and how are these positions different from Perry's epistemological positions?"

If women "make different sense of their experience" and construct knowledge differently from men, might women not write differently as well? Elizabeth A. Flynn concludes that in narrative writing, at least, they do. In "Composition as a Woman," Flynn analyzes the narratives of four students (two males and two females), discovering that the females' narratives were characterized by interaction, connection, or frustrated connection while the males' were characterized by separation, achievement, or frustrated achievement (428).

Here critical readers might wonder whether the author has exaggerated Flynn's conclusions. After all, many scholars are reluctant to assume a universal truth based on a sample size of four. In addition, academicians would probably want to hear more about how Flynn judged the female narratives as "characterized by interaction," etc.

the syntax and word choice without being aware of it, so it truly makes sense to take a second look at the original source. Taking three or more words from a secondary source amounts to more than sloppy scholarship: it is plagiarism. Naturally, you should also ensure that you have not misrepresented the secondary source by omitting the context or crucial qualifiers from the direct quote or in your paraphrased statement.

INTRODUCE THE CONTEXT AND CREDIBILITY OF REFERENCES

Academicians expect scholars to provide some background information about the research studies that they review. Without this information, readers may be unsure about the value of the reviewed studies. In Figure 15.1, extracted from a draft of one of my students' dissertation proposals, note how the lack of content development causes awkward transitions between ideas and undercuts the author's credibility. Because the author fails to give the necessary background about the studies she reviews, her discussion seems choppy and illogical. Many of the problems in this passage could be solved by a brief introduction concisely summarizing each scholar's credentials and research methods. Introductions of this sort are also crucial in highlighting exactly when you are incorporating someone else's ideas into your discussion.

With the hopes of swaying a reader, gifted rhetoricians sometimes intentionally avoid clarifying the context of research studies that they cite to support their positions. In his critique of higher education, *ProfScam: Professors and the Demise of Higher Education*, note how Charles Sykes fails to explain how Finn reached his conclusion that only one in ten professors makes significant contributions. By rushing on in his argument with the playful comment "he was being charitable," Sykes avoids a thoughtful discussion of how a significant contribution is defined, how scholars build on past essays as they mature, and how many studies Finn made before reaching his damning conclusion:

The debate over higher education often pits teaching versus research. But that begs the question, because it presupposes that the professors really do as much research as they claim and that the research they do actually has value. . . .

But how much research is really being done? And is it worth anything? Assistant Secretary of Education Chester Finn posed those same questions a few years back, before he went to work for the government. Of the 850,000 working academics in the country, Finn asked, how many really make any contribution to the "enlargement of human knowledge"? After eliminating the "horde of papers, articles, and books whose publication or presentation accomplished nothing save, perhaps, for the author's curricula vitae," Finn estimated that the answer would be that only 1 in 10 professors makes any contribution at all.[2]

He was being charitable. But Finn was highlighting one of the most embarrassing facts in the academic culture. Although the assumption that professors are busily at work on the frontiers of knowledge is the justification for their featherweight teaching loads, 60 percent of all college faculty members have never written or edited a book and one-third have never published even a single journal article.[3]

To his credit, we must acknowledge that Sykes does provide footnotes for Finn's assertion that few professors write and that the bulk of what they write is garbage. By turning to footnote two at the back of the book, the reader is provided with the following reference:

   2. Finn, Chester, "Higher Education on Trial: An Indict-
      ment," *Current*, October 1984.

In turn, Sykes provides the following reference for his assertion that professors carry "featherweight teaching loads" and that "60 percent of all college faculty members have never written or edited a book and one-third have never published even a single journal article."

3. Isoue, Robert, "How Colleges Can Cut Costs," *Wall Street Journal*, January 27, 1987.

Publication of these conclusions in a significant newspaper such as the *Wall Street Journal* or a periodical like *Current* establishes some credibility. Note, however, the absence of page numbers for these references and it's clear that a good amount of research will be needed to determine how reliable Finn's and Isoue's assertions are. Because few readers are willing to give hours to researching the authenticity of evidence, it is usually best to provide some background information when making controversial assertions.

For example, when reading the excerpt from Finn cited above, critical academic readers would want to know whether Finn read all of the "horde of papers, articles, and books" that the 850,000 working academics published. If so, how many years did this task take? If he reviewed a sample of these scholars' work, what steps did he take to ensure that it represented trends in the population? Did he limit his database to 85,000 papers, articles, and books published in 1983? What criteria did he use to evaluate the quality of the scholars' work? What has prepared Finn to evaluate manuscripts from such diverse disciplines as physics, mathematics, medicine, and engineering? Is Finn a scholarly author or an established editor of a scholarly journal?

Perhaps the most important question a critical reader might ask is, "Did Finn evaluate the evolution of each scholar's work over time?" After all, given the generative nature of language, it seems reasonable to assume that weak essays can emerge into stronger ones or help scholars improve as writers and researchers. The point has often been made, for example, that Darwin's early monographs on barnacle taxonomy (written between the ages of 37 and 45) hardly reflected the brilliant mind that would later reshape our conception of human evolution (Diamond; Boyer).

In turn, critical academic readers would have greater faith in Isoue's 1987 statistics if more background information about the sampling methodology were provided. Ultimately, however, many academic readers would dismiss the results of even a statistically valid average of "all college faculty members" on the basis that community college professors have different responsibilities than university professors at research institutions. Ultimately, few academic readers, I suspect, would consider the community college professor's 5-5 teaching load to be a featherweight load.

POWER QUOTE TO ESTABLISH A PERSUASIVE PERSONA

One of the conventions for introductions is to bow to predecessors and acknowledge your indebtedness to their ground-breaking, seminal research. If space limitations prohibit you from discoursing at length on the various works that contributed to your thinking on a subject, you can gather them together under the umbrella of a general, inclusive statement, as demonstrated in the samples below:

> A number of researchers (Bellack, Kliebard, Hyman, & Smith 1966; Cazden, John, & Hymes, 1972; Barnes, 1969; Flanders, 1979; Sinclair & Coulthard, 1978) have analyzed the language of classrooms and have come to the common conclusion that students have access to a limited number of language functions. (Gere and Abbott 374–375)

> In recent years, several reader response theorists (Bleich, 1975, 1978; Culler, 1975; Fish, 1970, 1976a, 1976b; Holland, 1973, 1975a, 1975b; Rosenblatt, 1976, 1978) have explored the unique role of the reader in the literary experience. Among the variety of explanations for the respective roles of the reader and text in the creation of meaning, some studies have demonstrated that readers' cognitive frameworks and psychological predispositions affect their response to literature (Applebee, 1975, 1976a, 1976b; Holland, 1975b; Kuehn, 1974; Peters & Blues, 1978; Petrosky, 1976; Thompson, 1974). (Hynds 386)

While power quoting can be an effective way to highlight important information, you can sometimes be more concise by citing one or two important studies. Also, check to ensure that the scholars and studies that you have grouped together truly support the statement you have made. If informed readers believe that you have bundled together studies that actually disagree in their conclusions or that don't truly support the assertion you have made, you will lose credibility no matter how strong the rest of your argument is.

COPYRIGHT LAW

Thanks to the revision of the copyright law in 1978, your writing is *immediately* covered. For instance, if you work on a book for several years, the latest draft of the book and any copies you make of it will be considered copyrighted for your life and for fifty years after your death. Because most academics write manuscripts for relatively small audiences and do not expect significant financial compensation, they understandably may not worry about copyrighting material. However, because you will have an easier time proving in court that a potentially lucrative manuscript or idea was yours if it is copyrighted, you may want to register it with the Copyright Office, which generally costs $10 for each application. To get the necessary forms, write to the Register of Copyrights, Copyright Office, Library of Congress, Washington, D.C. 20559.

Once a manuscript is published, the publisher will need to register it with the Copyright Office. Moreover, published documents should present the copyright notice, which includes the word "Copyright," the copyright symbol (©), the year of publication, and the name of the owner of the copyright, as illustrated below:

Copyright © 1991 Thomas Jefferson

Because unpublished manuscripts are still copyrighted without the copyright notice, you need not place the notice on your drafts of incomplete final products. Doing so is not only unnecessary, it may give the editor the sense that you don't trust him or her.

FAIR USAGE

Unlike the guidelines for establishing copyright, the rules for preserving "fair usage" are subject to debate and litigation. As demonstrated in the following excerpt from the copyright law, no specific word-length guidelines are given for what constitutes fair usage:

> In determining whether the use made of a work in any particular case is a fair use the factors to be considered shall include—
>
> (1) the purpose and character of the use, including whether such use is of commercial nature or is for nonprofit educational purposes;
> (2) the nature of the copyrighted work;
> (3) the amount and substantiality of the portion used in relation to the copyrighted work as a whole; and
> (4) the effect of the use upon the potential market for or value of the copyrighted work.

Because these guidelines are vague, publishers differ in how many words can be quoted without requiring permissions. A line of poetry or music lyrics, tables, illustrations, graphs, photographs, unpublished personal letters and diaries, company-prepared memos and letters to shareholders, interviews—these sorts of documents typically require permissions before a reputable publisher is willing to print them. If you take a line of a song or poem and reprint it without requesting permission from the copyright owner, for instance, you may end up in the courtroom, watching your life savings go toward a lawyer's new Porsche.

While a journal editor with a limited audience may allow 500 words to be cited, a textbook publisher with a large audience may require permission for 300 words or more. In its guidelines for authors, Greenwood Publishing Group offers the following suggestions:

Most publishers in the United States and Britain allow a certain amount of copyrighted prose or tabular material to be published without their written permission. It is considered "fair use" to quote this material—up to a total of 300 words—without fear of infringement. If the length of the original work is short, however (for example, an article or a newspaper report under copyright), the proportion of your quoted material to the length of the source is more important than the exact number of words that you have quoted. If you use more than a total of 300 words of direct quotation (in one place or scattered throughout the manuscript), from a single copyrighted work, you must seek formal copyright permission from the copyright owner.

Frankly, the only time you can be absolutely sure that you will not be infringing on someone's copyright is when you quote government documents or material that was published more than seventy-five years ago. Otherwise, when in doubt, be sure to request permission.

If numerous permissions will be called for in a book, you might also want to negotiate that the publisher will pay for them so that you avoid out-of-pocket expenses or losing your advance. If you are expected to get the copyright permissions, you should check with your publisher to ensure that you use the publisher's standard boilerplate for permissions.

ACKNOWLEDGE YOUR SUPPORTERS

The last step in the production of an academic manuscript is clearly the most enjoyable: acknowledging your supporters. Authors of articles often acknowledge their supporters in a footnote. In turn, authors of books may have an entire page of acknowledgments in which they thank review readers, colleagues, and friends who made the book possible. Although as a general rule you cannot go wrong thanking your friends and colleagues, it does make sense to share with them your acknowledgments before they are published to avoid upsetting them. For example, I once thanked a colleague with a passage that went something like, "I particularly want to thank Professor X for his careful copy-editing of the manuscript. Professor X is every writer's fantasy: a careful reader with a critical eye." Perhaps because I wrote this acknowledgment in a hurry, it never occurred to me that Professor X would dislike being portrayed principally as a reader. Fortunately, I shared the acknowledgment with the professor, witnessed his immediate displeasure, and rewrote it in a way that delighted him, as hoped.

FINAL COMMENTS

While the bulk of our work as scholars is rightfully concerned with interesting, complex issues, we cannot ignore the conventions for documenting sources that are used in our discipline. When editors receive work that is poorly documented, they immediately question the author's qualifications and commitment to the submitted work. In contrast, properly prepared documents are a joy for editors: they mean that the editor won't have to write long letters to the author outlining all of the page numbers, journal issue numbers, and dates needed before the work can be published.

WORKS CITED

Boyer, Ernest. *Scholarship Reconsidered: Priorities of the Professoriate.* Princeton, N.J.: The Carnegie Foundation for the Advancement of Teaching, 1990.

Diamond, Jared. "Publish or Perish." *Discover* (July 1989): 96–101.

Gere, Anne Ruggles, and Robert D. Abbott. "Talking about Writing: The Language of Writing Groups." *Research in the Teaching of English* 19 (December 1985): 362–382.

Hynds, Susan D. "Interpersonal Cognitive Complexity and the Literary Response Processes of Adolescent Readers." *Research in the Teaching of English* 19 (December 1985): 386–402.

Sykes, Charles J. *ProfScam: Professors and the Demise of Higher Education.* Washington, D.C.: Regnery Gateway, 1988.

Part III

How to Revise and Edit Your Work

16

How to Attack Manuscripts Like an Editor or Reviewer

There is a striking difference between scholarly publishing and most other social activities: *rejection is the rule in scholarly publication, not the exception.* The best journals—the ones scholars must publish in for tenure and promotion at research universities—often boast rejection rates of 95 percent. If a journal isn't tough to get into, then it may be discounted by a faculty member's department. In contrast, if someone truly dislikes you in your department, it would be highly unlikely for him or her to turn to you at a faculty meeting and say, "Sorry, your idea is not important. If you think of something worthwhile in the future, we would be glad to consider it." In any case, even the rudest of colleagues could not get away with this dismissive behavior 95 percent of the time!

Nevertheless, it is very commonplace for critics to attack manuscripts with the tenacity of a bulldog with rabies. When it comes to evaluating your own writing or implementing the harsh criticisms of review readers, you need to have especially thick skin. Naturally, you do not necessarily need to accept every criticism, but you should consider all of them seriously no matter how quirky they at first appear to be. Rather than getting depressed that your manuscript did not render your readers speechless over your rhetorical abilities, you may want to take cheer in the finding that revision is crucial to most writers. Even professional writers routinely need to revise their manuscripts to account for the insights of critics.

Academic writing is distinguished from most other kinds of writing in the degree of revision expected. While you can knock off a quick memo in a single draft, most academic essays require multiple revisions, some as many as a dozen or even four dozen. While tangled syntax and awkward wording may be acceptable in brief notes to colleagues, the rigorous peer-review process is designed to ensure that scholarly documents are exemplary. The high cost of scholarly publishing and the publisher's desire to attract highly educated readers require that only the best manuscripts be published. As guardians of the word, members of the professoriate are expected to write elegantly, to offer original contributions, and to help their disciplines evolve.

Rather than considering revision to be a relatively unimportant activity, like minor housekeeping, you can have a more accurate sense of how professional writers perceive revision if you consider it more similar to major renovation in which you tear down walls, rip off the roof, and add turrets. While you may be particularly adept at identifying and correcting grammatical and mechanical problems, you should ignore these concerns when you first begin revising. The problem with investing time in copy-editing rough drafts is that the ideas expressed in the drafts may be unoriginal or inappropriate for your audience. After investing time in making the prosaic seem elegant, you may have difficulty discarding the draft altogether. At the very least, you have lost valuable time.

In this chapter, I provide an overview of the questions that most editors and review readers use to critique manuscripts. Of course, reading is not a simple process in which all academicians ask the same questions and come up with the same answers. Different texts and occasions warrant emphasis on different questions. Yet academicians do share a number of conventions, and you should be aware that most editors and reviewers will consider these questions when critiquing your manuscripts.

Instead of considering all of these questions when critiquing your own or a colleague's manuscript, you may find it more useful to focus on one question or set of questions at a time. For instance, you may want to read through your manuscript once to ensure that you have conformed to the required documentation style. Second, don't get angry with yourself if you keep finding problems in even the tenth read-through. Instead, recognize that this *is* the process, that finding gaps in your thinking or having a sudden burst of inspiration that shatters your preconceptions is what makes the writing worth doing. Third, allow for as much incubation time as possible. We all need some distance from our ideas and drafts before we gain the perspective necessary to critique and develop them. Fourth, read your work out loud. In a surprisingly powerful way, this highlights problems with voice, content development, and grammar. Because of this, many writers mumble to themselves while they compose, and almost all successful writers read their final draft aloud to ensure that it is as effective as possible. Try it. You'll be surprised by its usefulness. Finally, to second-guess the editors and reviewers, you may wish to share drafts of your manuscripts with colleagues, asking them to evaluate them with a few of these questions in mind.

1. Is the subject truly significant and worthwhile?

   - What original contributions am I making to the literature?
   - Have I clarified for the reader what is significant about my results or ideas?

2. Have I thoroughly accounted for the intended audience?

   - Has my opinion about my audience changed as a result of writing?
   - Have I thoroughly accounted for what the readers need to know? What terms or concepts need clarification?

- Are my examples and illustrations effective? Should I provide more examples to help readers visualize conceptual problems? Have I used concepts that my readers will not understand?

- Have I introduced information that may make the audience angry? Can I eliminate these hot passages and still get my point across?

3. Have I established the tone most appropriate for the audience and purpose?

- Have I established the voice that I set out to present? Are there any sections in which I appear confused, pedantic, or angry?

- Now that I have thought more deeply about the subject, how have my thoughts changed about the particular voice that I should try to establish?

4. How have my thoughts on the subject developed as a result of writing?

- As I look over the whole, the paragraphs, the sentences, and the words, can I find ideas that have emerged through writing?

- Did I finish with the same purpose that I began with? What changes to my introduction need to be made to account for what I have actually done?

5. Are there any gaps in content development and reasoning?

- Do I need to provide additional reasoning or outside documentation to support controversial statements?

- Have I provided enough background information for readers to understand the discussion and evaluation?

- Have I addressed all of the important counter-arguments the reader is likely to consider? Have I cited the a apppropriate studies and relied on up-to-date information?

- If I am writing a research report, is there a clear connection between the problem and the methods, the results, and the conclusions? Have I exaggerated my position or results?

6. Is the rationale well developed?

- Will the audience be likely to be skeptical about the methods I have followed? Have I provided the references needed to support the method?

- Have I provided the details about the materials and methods employed needed to replicate the study?

- Have I talked too much about the methods employed and too little about the results? Are readers likely to think I am hiding something?

7. Is the document organized effectively?

- What is the overall organizing principle of the document? Am I organizing by topic and priority, by chronological order, by cause and effect? Have I organized my material deductively or inductively? Am I working from a problem to a solution or from a cause to an effect? Will another arrangement of the material be more effective?

- Throughout the text, have I moved from what the reader knows—*the given*—to what the reader doesn't know—*the new*?

- Have I provided the forecasting and transitional sentences that readers will need to understand how the different ideas relate to each other?

- Is my manuscript unified and energized by a compelling purpose, or does it seem to wander from subject to subject?

- When describing *what* something is, have I effectively ranked the issues in their order of importance?

- When explaining *how* something occurred, have I divided the issue or process into major steps?

- When explaining *why*, have I thoroughly explored all possible causes and effects? Have I confused coincidental relationships for causal ones?

8. Have I established a professional style?

  - Can I cut the length of the document in half? Have I really tried to edit for economy?

  - Are any of the examples and illustrations unnecessary given the audience's level of knowledge? Are any examples and illustrations redundant?

9. Have I followed the conventions for documenting sources?

Have I acknowledged indebtedness to all of the scholars whose original ideas I used when developing the document?

  - Is it clear when I am using outside sources? Are quotation marks placed around short quotations, and are longer quotations placed in block quote format?

  - Have I established the credibility of the sources? For example, when reviewing other scholars' research findings, have I clarified their methods so that my readers can better judge their reliability?

  - Have I accurately paraphrased relevant sources?

  - Am I using too many secondary references? Can I make my document stronger by paraphrasing some of the direct quotes? Has my research material overcome my voice and purpose?

  - Will I need to obtain permission to cite any sources? Have I followed "fair use" guidelines? (See Chapter 15 for a discussion of copyright laws.)

10. Are the paragraphs coherent and cohesive?

  - Are paragraphs in the most effective order in the text?

- Should the existing paragraphs be cut into smaller segments or merged into longer ones?

- Should a later paragraph—say the third paragraph—be combined with an introductory paragraph?

- Will readers understand the logical connections between paragraphs? Are additional sentences needed to clarify the logical relationship between ideas?

- Have I been too blatant about transitions? Are all of the transitional sentences and paragraphs really necessary, or can the reader follow my thoughts without them?

11. Is the document formatted effectively?

- Can I use a picture, a graph, or a table to represent my meaning visually?

- Are all of the visuals necessary? Am I offering simple-to-understand concepts or repeating information that is already presented concisely in the text?

- Would my material be more readable if I boldfaced major and minor subheadings?

- Have I followed the requirements of the journal or book publisher to which I will submit the work?

- What changes in the format of my document will make my prose more readable? Should I use fewer or more subheadings? Can I use bullets, subheadings, or lists to emphasize key points?

FINAL COMMENTS

Once you have addressed the substantive issues posed by these questions, you are ready to attack your sentences like a copy editor. The next chapter covers readability guidelines for ensuring that your sentences are precise, emphatic, and concise. Before tearing your document apart at the sentence level, however, you might

want to take a moment to admire it. Although I might sound
facetious here, I am truly quite serious: you should balance criticism with praise, and remember that all documents—even those
written by world-renowned scholars—have faults. Writing well
can be a difficult activity, so you need to reward yourself from time
to time.

17

How to Edit Documents Like a Copy Editor

Once you believe a draft conveys the information you want your readers to understand, you can begin attacking it at the sentence level. After working hard to develop a manuscript, you understandably may be weary of it and eager to send it out for review. If possible, set the document aside and work on another project before trying to copy-edit it. If the due date is upon you, however, the following techniques may help you critically evaluate the document at the sentence level:

1. Don't try to copy-edit a document all at once. Instead, alternate proofreading with other activities.

2. Three useful strategies can help you ignore the content of a message and concentrate on grammatical, mechanical, and formatting errors. First, try reading your document backwards. Second, place sheets of paper above and below each sentence in the document as you read through it. Third, place slashes between each sentence.

3. If you are using a personal computer, try printing the document with a different font, such as size 14 or size 16 instead of size 12.

4. Look for clusters of mistakes. When you find one error in paragraph seven, for example, carefully examine the surrounding sentences to see if you had a lapse of concentration when you wrote and copy-edited that section.

5. Look for errors you often make, such as errors in pronoun agreement or subject-verb agreement.

Now, just as you limited the number of substantive questions when revising your document, you should limit the editorial issues you consider when copy-editing. For example, rather than considering all eight of the following editorial concerns when evaluating a nearly final draft, you may want to read the manuscript with the first three strategies in mind, take a break, and then read it again while keeping another three copy-editing concerns in mind.

1. Avoid unnecessary jargon and awkward abstractions.

2. Use the first person.

3. Use the active rather than the passive voice.

4. Limit use of *to be* verbs.

5. Select an appropriate sentence length and sentence pattern.

6. Maintain a high verb-to-noun ratio and avoid nominalizations.

7. Edit strings of prepositional phrases.

8. Edit for economy.

9. Copy-edit for grammatical, mechanical, and formatting errors.

AVOID UNNECESSARY JARGON AND
AWKWARD ABSTRACTIONS

Because academic journals cater to narrow audiences, their use of jargon is somewhat justified. Specialists, after all, use jargon as a form of shorthand to enhance communication. Rather than belaboring seminal research or theories, experienced academics cite relevant scholars, studies, or philosophical movements to call to mind related assumptions and past research.

It is also true that some journals cater to narrow audiences that delight in playful word combinations and obscure jargon, so a prospective author needs to master this discourse before becoming a member of the club. For instance, an avid reader of literature who nonetheless lacks training in critical theory would find most essays published in *PMLA*, the journal of the Modern Language Association, to be impenetrable and undecipherable. As an example, try translating the following introduction to a recent essay in *PMLA*:

In *S/Z* Roland Barthes repeatedly articulates a tripartite structure as the basic grammar of the classic realist text. In outlining a homological relation between language and discourse, for example, he projects the sentence as the image of narrative order: it presents a subject to be developed, subordinate clauses that add complexity, and a conclusion that coincides with complete predication. On this framework, which he calls a question-delay-answer schema (4–86, 126–28), he improvises a remarkable sequence of variations. Thus a topographical model posits the quest as the regulatory trope: first a departure, next a "temporary wandering of the predicate," and then the return that marks the end of the journey (187–88). In the biological model, an impregnation, which plants the seed of discourse, is followed by "a kind of pregnancy for its full term" and ultimately by the birth of new meaning (62). The dominant model, however—the one on which Barthes conducts his analysis of Balzac's "Sarrasine"—is the hermeneutic one: the classic realist text begins by formu-

lating an enigma, an "insufficient half truth, powerless to
name itself," a mystery caught up "in the initial void of its
answer."

In this excerpt, the author uses jargon and plays with language and
metaphor to establish his credentials with the literary community.
Those who lack years of training in critical theory may find the
passage impenetrable. One wonders, "Can't it be said more simply?"

Recent critics of higher education, such as Page Smith, have
ridiculed academese while asserting that the tendency toward
specialization and the rat race for original material are undermining
our responsibility to write clearly for broad, less educated audiences. All of the great stylists of our time—Claire Kehrwald Cook,
Joseph Williams, William Strunk and E. B. White—encourage
authors to eschew jargon when possible. And some prominent
academic editors, such as Robert Day, have challenged us to
eliminate unnecessary jargon from our professional journals:

> Much of today's academic writing is turgid to the point of
> being incomprehensible to all except a small coterie. This is
> all right if the publication is designed for only that coterie.
> However, shouldn't most scholarly publications be written
> for an audience of reasonable size, an audience including not
> only peers of the author but also specialists reading outside
> their own narrow discipline, students trying hard to master
> the material needed to join the coterie, and peers whose native
> language is other than English? (113)

Rather than priding themselves on simplifying the complex, many
scholars seem to take great delight in complicating the simple. In
a recent analysis of the gulf between academic and trade language,
Chris Goodrich writes:

Fifty years ago, scholars and book editors shared the same general background and the same general view of the world; although neither objected if a book sold many copies and made the author famous, they wrote and published primarily to reach like-minded people. As times changed, however, so, dramatically, did the genteel academic/publisher compact. Conglomerates swallowed up individual publishers, who in turn became more and more oriented to the bottom line; academics became ever more specialized, careerist, and bound to the forms and language of their chosen disciplines. The publishing and academic paths, once parallel, diverged until they were separated by a yawning gulf. Editors began to regard academics as constitutionally incapable of writing well or addressing broad topics; scholars saw that trade publishing was suffering from what came to be known as the "block-buster complex." (17)

Although most professors would be insulted by Page Smith's and Charles Sykes's misrepresentation of academic life,[1] we still need to address their reasonable criticisms of academese. Yes, jargon can provide an invaluable shorthand among specialists. It is, for example, unreasonable to expect science writers to communicate clearly to nonscientists when they are reporting their research in academic journals. Even science magazines that attract broad audiences, such as *Science* and the *New England Journal of Medicine*, require some technical training. However, as Day and others have argued, we do have a responsibility to communicate clearly to our students and others interested in how our disciplines are evolving. We need to recognize that the readability and grace of our prose diminish with the use of needless abstractions and excessive jargon. Rather than solely addressing narrow audiences of insiders in professional journals, we should consider our responsibilities to less informed audiences. Further, much jargon—even among specialists—is merely a smoke screen for fuzzy thinking.

USE THE FIRST PERSON

The American Psychological Association (APA) guidelines—
pretty much the style bible for most academic publications in
the social and natural sciences—have been saying bluntly
since 1973 that scientists should speak in the first person as
"I" or "we" in their publications if they are telling their own
conclusions or describing their own experimental proce-
dures. And yet many scientists persist in telling their students
and themselves that it is wrong to use the first person in
academic writing. Even academics in the humanities tend to
shy away from much use of the first person—certainly using
it much less than if they were writing a memo to the same
colleagues about these same topics.—Peter Elbow

"Do not use the first person" is perhaps the most pernicious
recommendation that English teachers make. After all, how can
we think without using our experience? Why must we drive a stake
through our cerebral cortex before writing? How can we logically
assume that we are more objective thinkers when we avoid the first
person? As an example, what sort of persona do you infer from
reading the following passage from an essay in *Evaluation and*
Program Planning?

While some evaluation specialists disagree (Scriven, 1973)
this writer believes that a well-planned evaluation effort
begins with clearly established goals. Sometimes goals are
established by the program staff along with the evaluator well
in advance of the program and the planned evaluation. This
is the "best case" scenario (Posavac & Carey, 1984). However, in the case of the Very Special Arts Evaluation, programs were already in operation in many locales and had been
running for a long period of time. Therefore, it was not
possible for the author to be involved in the goal establish-
ment process. In fact, one of the first questions this evaluator
posed to Very Special Arts focused on the goals and criteria

> that were to be the benchmark against which Very Special Arts programs were to be evaluated.

Can you see that the author's prose could be more vigorous, less pedantic, if he used the first person, as suggested by the following revision?

> While I would have preferred to establish goals for evaluating the Very Special Arts programs before their inception, I was unable to do so because the programs already had been operating for three years in ten cities. Nevertheless, I was able to develop effective evaluative criteria by meeting with personnel from each of the arts programs and discussing their goals.

Now, it is true that use of the first person can be obtrusive. In the bulk of writing that we do as academics, readers care more about the information and the ideas than about us as authors. (Right now, for example, I'm assuming that you don't care that I'm rather tired after getting up with my child at 4:45 A.M. You are not concerned that she may wake up if I risk making a pot of coffee. Yet when stating an opinion or offering an overview of the goals of a section or chapter, I may as well be straightforward and admit that these are *my* opinions or goals. After all, I can create confusion by avoiding the first person and hiding behind passive-voice sentences.)

USE THE ACTIVE RATHER THAN THE PASSIVE VOICE

Essentially, a verb is *passive* when its subject is acted upon by an outside agent rather than doing the action. You can identify the passive voice by finding a sentence that uses some form of the verb *to be* (*am, is, was, were, being, been*) along with a *past participle* (a verb form often ending in -*ed* or -*en*). The preposition *by* usually follows the *to be* verb and the past participle, or it can be implied, as illustrated below:

Passive: The data were confirmed.
Active: Three independent scholars confirmed the data.

Passive: I was made a better scholarly author by writing regularly.
Active: Writing regularly has made me a better scholarly author.

Passive: She was had by the con man.
Active: The con man had her.

Passive sentences tend to be wordy, dull, and confusing. They leave readers unsure of who or what is causing the action. Nine times out of ten, you should transform passive sentences into active ones. Surprisingly, however, the use of the passive voice is endemic in academic discourse, particularly in the methods section of quantitative research reports. Notice how the following excerpt from an essay in *Philosophical Magazine A* becomes more vigorous and concise once it is transformed into the active voice:

Passive: In this paper the contrast of dislocations in icosahedral quasicrystals is discussed in the framework of the quasilattice model and on the basis of the kinematical theory of electron diffraction. Since, at present, little is known about the structure of quasicrystal dislocations, our treatment is restricted to the derivation of conditions under which the diffraction contrast vanishes and the dislocations become invisible. Some basic structural properties of quasilattices and quasilattice dislocations are first discussed.
Active: We discuss the contrast of dislocations in icosahedral quasicrystals in the framework of the quasilattice model and on the basis of the kinematical theory of electron diffraction. We restrict our treatment to the derivation of conditions under which the diffraction contrast vanishes and the dislocations become invisible because we know little about the structure

of quasicrystal dislocations. First we discuss some basic structural properties of quasilattices and quasilattice dislocations.

While the passive voice strangles the life from most academic discourse, it does have some legitimate uses. For example, in a description of course requirements, you might want to say, *Active class participation and an oral presentation of at least one research project will also be required,* so that you emphasize active participation rather than yourself, as the active form would do—that is, *I will require active participation and one oral presentation from you.*

LIMIT USE OF TO BE *VERBS*

In our daily speech and rough drafts, we tend to rely heavily on the various forms of the verb *to be.* Beyond being boring because of its overuse, the verb *to be* is unlike any other verb because it is *inert*—that is, it doesn't show any action. For example, in the sentence *"The researcher is a professor at Duke,"* the verb *is* merely connects the subject with what grammarians call the *subject complement.* We could just as easily say *"A professor at Duke is the researcher"* without changing the meaning of the sentence.

It would be nearly impossible to draft documents without some linking verbs. Yet because you diminish the vigor of a manuscript by using *is* and *are* constructions, you should try to limit their frequency. Finally, note that the *progressive* form of a linking verb, which involves using *to be* as an auxiliary verb with a participle, is not nearly as pernicious as the endemic *is* or *are.* The progressive form has the advantage of illustrating action as it progresses over time, thereby enabling us to shape concise sentences indicating that something is currently happening: *The coauthors are disagreeing about the order in which their names should be listed when the book is published.*

It is and *there are* constructions often lead to sluggish, passive sentences, so you should eliminate most of them from your documents. Sentences like *It is clearly a fact that the so and so did not invent cold fusion* can invariably be improved by eliminating the weak beginning.

> *Sample*: While it is crucial for us to speak out on behalf of education, it is important that we do so in a manner consistent with statute and administrative rule.
> *Revision*: We need to speak out on behalf of education while observing statute and administrative rules.

> *Sample*: According to the certification theory, there is no intrinsic relation between creativity and IQ.
> *Revision*: Certification theory posits no intrinsic relation between creativity and IQ.

You should not, however, attempt to eliminate all *it is* or *there are* constructions. You may, for example, want to occasionally use these constructions to establish an impersonal tone or to avoid repeating a subject at the beginning of the sentence.

SELECT AN APPROPRIATE SENTENCE LENGTH AND SENTENCE PATTERN

Long sentences are not necessarily ineffective or wordy, nor are short sentences necessarily concise. After all, a seventy-word sentence, properly constructed, can clarify relationships between ideas, while a series of five-word sentences can create a choppy style and fail to make logical connections between ideas. Rather than making all sentences a certain length, you can write gracefully by being aware of the demands different sentence patterns make on readers.

Place the Subject At or Near the Beginning of the Sentence

As a general rule, you can make your prose more readable by limiting the number of words that come between the beginning of a sentence and its subject. To make the beginning of a sentence emphatic, you should generally avoid cluttering it with unnecessary transitional words or phrases. A second problem with long introductory phrases and clauses is that they strain the reader's short-term memory. Notice, for example, how you need to juggle all of the following conditions in your short-term memory until you come to the end of the sentence:

> If you write every morning for at least fifteen minutes, if you set aside the urge to criticize early drafts and ideas, if you analyze the rhetorical situation for a document, if you ask critical questions of your drafts, if you share drafts with colleagues, then you will improve as a writer.

Fortunately, most sentences with long introductory clauses can be easily improved; one need only move the concluding words—that is, the independent clause—to the beginning of the sentence, as in the following revision:

> You will improve as a writer if you write every morning for at least fifteen minutes, if . . . ideas, if . . . document, if . . . drafts, if . . . colleagues.

When copy-editing sentences, you should not attempt to eliminate all of the introductory words, phrases, and clauses. A few introductory clauses can help establish a forceful rhythm, and you would put your readers to sleep if all of the sentences were shaped in the same way. Occasional transitional words or phrases can also aid readability. *Therefore, however, on the other hand, as a result*—these sorts of words, if used selectively and logically, can highlight how different ideas relate to each other. Nevertheless, such words and phrases cannot create logical connections by themselves. Just as a brick house would collapse if the builder used sand rather than mortar to construct it, so will meaning in a document if you do not provide a logical discussion.

Avoid Excessive Embedding between the Subject and Verb

Embedding appositives or modifiers between subjects and verbs can enliven what is traditionally considered the least emphatic part of a sentence, the middle. Notice, for example, how the appositive in the following example emphasizes the definition of *sentence combining*:

> Research suggests that sentence combining, an instructional technique that provides students with practice, is effective in developing writers, elementary through college level.

If we wanted to give less emphasis to the definition of sentence combining, we could recast the sentence as follows:

> Research with elementary- through college-level writers suggests that practice combining sentences promotes syntactical fluency.

You should use this pattern sparingly, however. Embedding an appositive, a participle phrase, or a relative clause[2] between the subject and the verb slows down the pace of reading because such constructions require readers to keep these references in their short-term memory until they reach the verb and understand how to apply them. As English speakers we need to link the subject of a sentence to its verb to understand a statement. As a result, we must hold in our short-term memory all of the defining and modifying words that come between the subject and verb. Not until we reach the verb do we understand what we are supposed to do with the appositive or modifying words.

MAINTAIN A HIGH VERB-TO-NOUN RATIO AND AVOID NOMINALIZATIONS

You can invigorate your language by eliminating unnecessary nouns and choosing powerful verbs. When editing, consider changing

Latinized nouns—those ending with *ance*, *ing*, *ion*, *tion*, or *ment*—into verbs. For example, transform *introduction* into *introduce*; *commitment* into *commit*; *feeling* into *feel*. Changing nouns into verbs can produce a more concise and vigorous passage, as illustrated below:

Sample: The assumption that creative ability has a relationship to intelligence warrants further examination.
Revision: We must examine how creative ability relates to intelligence.

Sample: This introduction is a rough conception of the assumptions about the decision-making process underlying the conception: Decisions about belief or action generally occur in the context of some problem and have some basis.
Revision: We can assume that decisions occur in response to problems.

EDIT STRINGS OF PREPOSITIONAL PHRASES

When used in moderation, prepositions are invaluable. Few sentences can be written without them. Essentially, prepositions work as connectors, linking the object of the preposition to a word that appears earlier in the sentence. Like linking verbs, however, prepositions do not convey action, nor do they subordinate one thought to another. Instead, they merely link chunks of meaning that readers must gather together in order to understand the sentence. When used excessively, prepositional phrases create a choppy, listlike style. Consider, for instance, the following sentence excerpted from the *Journal of Research and Development in Education*:

Sample: The major objective of this study was to determine the perceived effects of the union on monetary and on non-monetary aspects of compensation over the period in which respondents to the survey had been union members.

Because it occurs in the conclusion of a five-page published essay, a careful editor would probably have eliminated this sentence altogether. Let's face it: if the readers still haven't got the point after five pages, there is little hope for them. Nevertheless, if the editor and author believed this statement was necessary, they could improve the sentence by reducing the number of prepositions:

> *Revision*: This study examines how the union affects monetary and nonmonetary aspects of compensation.

To help identify and eliminate unnecessary prepositions, you may find it useful to put slashes between the various prepositional phrases and other basic sentence parts. Note, for example, how the slashes in the following sentence, which is excerpted from the *Journal of Research and Development in Education*, highlight the frequency of prepositional phrases.

> /Furthermore,/ /in response/ /to the increased pressure/ /to publish/ /in academia/ /in the past decade/ /and the growing complexity/ /of the academic areas and research tools,/ /one should expect/ /to find/ /increased emphasis/ /on cost-cutting techniques/ /by academic writers./ /An increase/ /in cost/ /can probably be observed/ /by investigating/ /the changing trends/ /in the multiple authorship/ /of articles/ /over time./

EDIT FOR ECONOMY

No matter how much you appreciate the sounds of the words you have used, you should now try to cut the length of your document in half. By using the editing strategies already discussed, you have begun to chip away needless abstractions, unnecessary jargon, awkward passive constructions, weak verbs, tangled sentence patterns, unnecessary nouns, and strings of prepositional phrases. Yet by evaluating the content in light of your audience and the tone that you hope to establish, you can still find ways to eliminate unnecessary transitions, definitions, references, and examples. It may be useful at this point to recall that you add clarity and grace by presenting an idea simply. Cutting away at the unnecessary dead wood can eliminate the static that interferes with communication.

As an example of wordiness, consider the following excerpt from a recent issue of *Medical Teacher*. After an impenetrable abstract and two pages of academese that presumably introduce the topic, the coauthors of this article offered the first sense of their purpose for writing:

> The purpose of this paper is to present the results of a faculty development project in which the domain of written communication was analysed and incorporated into a training curriculum for family medicine faculty members. Funded by the Division of Medicine, Health Resources Services Administration, and directed by investigators at the University of Minnesota (Department of Family Practice and Community Health) and the University of North Carolina (Office of Research and Development for Education in the Health Professions), this two and a half year contract called for the development of a model curriculum to prepare physicians for their faculty roles in five areas. Written communication was one of the areas included for tenure-track faculty members, along with research, teaching, administration, and professional academic skills. In its entirety this curriculum is suitable for the continuing medical education, faculty development, or fellowship level.
>
> In order to prepare the written communication domain of this curriculum, an instructional analysis was performed on the content and context of written communication skills in academic medicine.

Presumably, this paragraph, which should appear much earlier in the article, is intended to clarify the purpose of the research. Instead of emphasizing the various funding agencies and universities that were involved, the authors should focus on the significance and scope of their research. I suspect, for instance, that most readers would appreciate the brevity and clarity of the following revision:

> The curriculum presented in this paper can help prepare family medicine physicians for faculty positions that require academic and administrative writing. This curriculum is also suitable for the continuing medical education and faculty development.

Financial supporters and home institutions can be acknowledged in a by-line or in a footnote. Because the current article does not deal with other aspects of their curriculum—research, teaching, administration, and professional academic skills—the authors should not mention these concerns (unless, of course, they want to refer readers to related articles or broaden the scope and length of their article).

The academese suffocating the authors' meaning in the preceding excerpt from *Medical Teacher*, written, ironically, by faculty members who teach other faculty members to write, is by no means unusual. In my survey of available literature, I found innumerable passages that could have worked equally well to make the above point.

In your search for economy and precision, you should delete unnecessary repetitions. Of course, you are understandably anxious to report everything necessary to help explain your opinion or argue persuasively. Yet by deleting redundant adjectives, repeated phrases, and synonyms, your writing will gain clarity and persuasiveness. Whenever possible, try to replace *abstract* words with *concrete* words—words that represent actual physical things like "chair" and "house"—and *sensory* words—words that appeal to people's five senses. This does not mean, however, that you need to go into monotonous detail about facts or concepts that your readers are likely to know. It does mean that you should critically evaluate every word you use, asking, "Will my reader(s) understand me here? Do I need to define these terms and concepts? What abstract words can I replace with details and specifics?"

An Exercise in Editing for Economy

To give you some practice at editing for economy, four excerpts from academic journals appear below, followed by my revisions. First try making your own revision, and then compare your text to mine.

Sample: In the middle 1970s, as some faculty members began to face a shrinking job market, the focus of faculty bargaining began the shift toward personnel matters, with faculty members expressing growing concern about job security, advancement and tenure policies.

Revision: The shrinking job market of the 1970s in some disciplines moved the focus of faculty bargaining to job security, advancement, and tenure policies.

Sample: As growing numbers of infertile heterosexual and gay and lesbian couples, along with single individuals, seek to parent through techniques that facilitate conception or permit the use of a genetic and/or gestational donor, and the boundaries of the "scientifically possible" enlarge, we are confronted with a host of increasingly urgent questions.

Revision: We are confronted with a host of increasingly urgent questions as the boundaries of the "scientifically possible" enlarge: growing numbers of single individuals and infertile heterosexual, gay, and lesbian couples are seeking to parent through techniques that facilitate conception or permit the use of a genetic and/or gestational donor.

Sample: The returns to academic publishing have been studied in recent articles by Katz (1973), Tuckman and Leahey (1975), and Tullock (1973). The returns on publishing are shown to range from psychic rewards such as increased reputation and status, to monetary and professional rewards such as salary increases, promotion and tenure, expanded career opportunities, and increased mobility. In measuring monetary and professional rewards, the cited authors have found evidence of diminishing marginal returns on academic publishing. Conversely, there are costs associated with academic writing. The monetary costs of academic publishing are to a large extent absorbed by the writer's university. The costs incurred by the writer are mainly personal. These costs can be measured in terms of the time and effort expended for researching and writing the article, lost professional opportunities such as lost outside consulting fees, and foregone leisure time. The nature of these costs are such that they will not diminish rapidly after the writer's research skills mature. In fact, costs may even be an increasing function of publishing, if lost consulting fees are related to professional reputation and professional reputation is an increasing function of publishing. Faced with such a cost return structure, it is apparent that the rational writer makes an economic decision each time he decides to write an article. The purpose of this paper will be to define the rational behavior of an academic writer. Once rational behavior is defined, it will be shown that this behavior is consistent with currently observed trends in academic publishing.

Revision: Academicians receive more monetary and professional rewards for working as consultants than as scholars once they have established their reputation and earned tenure.

Sample: Bowlby (1973, 1988a) perceives agoraphobic individuals as experiencing a chronic state of anxiety over the availability and responsiveness of their attachment figures. Because of their uncertainty and fear of desertion or worry that they may not be cared for, they seek to maintain proximity to assure contact with attachment figures. The apprehension about their relationships hampers their going forth into the world and also their coping with stressful conditions such as separation and loss when they do occur.

Revision: Bowlby (1973, 1988a) believes that agoraphobic individuals feel chronically anxious over the availability and responsiveness of their attachment figures. Their fear of desertion makes them stay close to their attachment figures, thereby hampering their going forth into the world and coping with stressful conditions.

COPY-EDIT FOR GRAMMATICAL, MECHANICAL, AND FORMATTING ERRORS

While you can depend on a journal's or publisher's copy editors to identify stylistic infelicities, you can establish yourself as a pro and a detail person by eliminating errors from your text. Now that you have attacked your document at the textual, paragraph, and sentence level, you should make one final search for errors in pronoun agreement, subject-verb agreement, punctuation, and spelling. Look especially for errors that reviewers and mentors commonly find in your writing. If you have questions about identifying these sorts of errors, I recommend Claire Kehrwald Cook's superb text, *Line by Line: How to Improve Your Own Writing* (New York: MLA, 1985).

FINAL COMMENTS

Taken in isolation, using each of the strategies discussed in this chapter may seem like nit-picking. Going through a document and reducing the number of linking verbs, for example, will not make a substantial difference in its readability. Yet, taken as a whole, these strategies can help you find the *truth*—the essence of what you want to express. Although at first these techniques may seem awkward or mechanical, once you have worked with them for a while they will become natural and automatic. The end result will be smooth prose that is a joy to read. After a while, you will apply these strategies without even thinking about them. Soon you will be editing everything you hear, from television commercials to editorials in the daily newspaper. Soon your colleagues will be coming to you for editorial help because somehow your work always seems so well written.

NOTES

1. For example, Page Smith leads readers to believe that professors commonly teach two to three classes a year, despise students, and are paid on average $80–100,000 per year. In turn, Charles Sykes portrays professors as Machiavellian figures who routinely sexually abuse their protégés, produce nothing but profspeak, and rarely teach. (See Chapter 18 for a more complete discussion of how critics have misrepresented problems in academia.)

2. As you may recall, an appositive is a word or phrase that renames or redefines a noun or pronoun; a participle is a verb form that functions as an adjective; and a relative clause, which usually begins with *that*, *who*, or *which*, is a dependent clause that offers additional information about a noun.

WORKS CITED

Day, Robert A. "The Development of Research Writing." *Scholarly Publishing* (January 1989): 107–115.

Goodrich, Chris. "Crossover Dreams: What Academics Need to Know about Agents and the Literary Marketplace." *Lingua Franca* (August 1991): 16–21.

Part IV

Current Issues and Emerging Possibilities

18

Where Can We Go from Here?

Throughout this book I have taken a decidedly positive view of scholarly publishing. As a writer and composition theorist, I am quick to celebrate the significance of the creative process. I know that writing stimulates thinking, imagination, and learning. I know that scholarly writing and publishing can be personally rewarding. I believe that we have a better chance of solving the problems confronting our society if we can involve more of our colleagues in research and scholarship. And on a solely practical level, I know that being active as scholars helps us serve as mentors to students. By being aware of what important conversations are taking place in scholarly publications, we can guide students toward original research projects and better understand research and writing problems that they confront.

While the techniques presented in this book can help scholars write more effectively and find publishers for their ideas, we also must recognize that some of our most gifted colleagues will turn away from our invitations to write and participate in scholarly discourse. Although books like this one can help active scholars and researchers write and publish more, they can be compared to yelling in a hurricane if the goal is perceived to be involving faculty who are not publishing their ideas or conducting research. Barring major improvements in our economic and political conditions, we have no reason to hope that more of the 85 or 90 percent of faculty who are now quiet will share their views by publishing them. If we are ever to involve more professors in scholarship, then we need to resolve the teaching versus scholarship debate, redefine what we mean by scholarship, and question how institutions, professional organizations, and faculty members can help encourage scholarship.

MUST WE CHOOSE BETWEEN TEACHING AND SCHOLARSHIP?

Recent critics of higher education have accused us of abandoning the classroom. In the media, we have been portrayed like an obsessive compulsive alcoholic who can identify only two choices: to drink excessively or stay stone sober; that is, critics often charge that we cannot teach well because of the terrific emphasis administrators place on publishing scholarship. For instance, Ernst L. Boyer, President of the Carnegie Foundation, has written elegantly that we need to reclaim teaching as an inspiring and significant responsibility. In *Scholarship Reconsidered*, Boyer argues that professors work hardest as scholars because they are not rewarded for effective classroom teaching:

> In the current climate, students all too often are the losers. . . .
> In the glossy brochures, they're assured that teaching is important, that a spirit of community moves the campus, and that general education is the core of the undergraduate experience. But the reality is that, on far too many campuses, teaching is not well rewarded, and faculty who spend too much time counseling and advising may diminish their prospects for tenure and promotion. (xi–xii)

In his survey of more than 5,000 faculty members, Boyer found that 52 percent of the respondents at four-year colleges and 14 percent at two-year institutions believed "observations of teaching by colleagues and/or administrators" to be "very unimportant" or "fairly unimportant" in determining who was granted tenure. Forty-four percent of his respondents at four-year institutions "disagreed with reservations" or "strongly disagreed" that "teaching effectiveness should be the primary criterion for promotion of faculty." In contrast, only 4 percent of the faculty at two-year colleges felt this way. As any academic knows from personal experience or from reading professional magazines and newspapers such as the *Chronicle of Higher Education*, these results are *not* surprising: after all, professors at four-year universities are expected to publish. Unlike their colleagues at two-year colleges, they are provided with course-load releases to conduct scholarly research. Instead of being expected to teach four or five sections each semester, they may have a three-two load, or if they are at a first-rate research institution, a two-two or a one-two load. Since they are expected to publish, it makes sense to evaluate their efforts at scholarship as much as their efforts at teaching.

However, it is important to note that 46 percent of the faculty at four-year institutions "strongly agree" or "agree with reservations" that "the pressure to publish reduces the quality of teaching at my university." In turn, 14 percent of the professors at two-year colleges feel this way. Because we cannot know how involved these faculty members are as scholars, we cannot conclude that they are necessarily correct in their assumption that time spent working as scholars detracts from their work in the classroom. It is possible, for instance, that many of these faculty members have never conducted any scholarship or that their contributions have been minimal. Perhaps they are simply angry about the professor down the hall who received a higher merit raise because of an influential book. After all, 13 percent of the faculty members at four-year institutions who responded to Boyer's survey have published no essays, and 30 percent of them have published one to five essays.

Even more damning was the finding that 49 percent of these respondents have written or edited no books. Naturally, fewer academics have published at two-year institutions: 52 percent had published no articles, and 69 percent had written or edited no books.

Yet, as any resident of California would be quick to tell us, *perception is reality*. No matter how sure we are of the benefits of scholarship and of the interrelationship between teaching and scholarship, we cannot afford to bury our heads in the sand, hoping that the critics of higher education will move along and find something else to critique.

It is, for instance, quite obvious to anyone remotely associated with higher education that professors are not rewarded for teaching well. It should not be surprising, therefore, that some faculty at research universities focus on research at the expense of teaching. When facing low salaries and few rewards for teaching, some professors work hard at chasing consulting contracts and grant money instead of focusing on their students' needs. And thanks to the luxury of tenure, some faculty members have just tuned out, turning their attention toward hobbies, TV, sports, and family. We all know a few professors who waste their students' time rather than teaching them. Although we lack statistics on faculty productivity—after all, objective assessments of quality are impossible to determine—we can guess that a good many faculty members have used tenure as a shield from working hard in the classroom, library, and lab.

The woeful lack of emphasis our society places on education tears at the heart of even the most cynical academicians. Throughout the country teachers are being asked to teach more and more students. It is not uncommon for lecture classes to have 300 students, making it unrealistic for faculty members to assign writing or essay tests. While professional organizations such as the National Council of Teachers of English and the Conference on College Composition and Communication argue in proclamation after proclamation that writing classes should be limited to fifteen students, these classes are getting larger and larger, moving toward twenty-five and thirty students in a section. If the current disregard for teaching continues, we will soon have two castes: the educated in private schools and the illiterate in dangerous public schools.

We college professors and secondary educators are certainly not responsible for our society's lack of concern for how we educate our people, so we shouldn't hold ourselves solely responsible for the literacy crisis or the epidemic of violence and poverty decaying our country. Yet we do need to work with our colleagues and administrators to reaffirm teaching as a fundamental and significant act at research universities. We need to step out of our classrooms and address our society's appalling lack of support for education. We can reward our colleagues who find their greatest joy in teaching as opposed to conducting research by acknowledging their efforts and accomplishments. And to offer our colleagues some extra time to conduct significant research, we can expect nonpublishing colleagues to maintain heavier teaching loads than colleagues who are involved heart and soul in scholarly endeavors. It certainly seems reasonable to me to expect academicians at the four-year level who are not engaged in research projects to have the same teaching load as professors at the two-year level. Yet these should be flexible tracks, not rigid publisher versus nonpublisher tracks. After all, we want to engage the imagination and intellect of all of our colleagues. Rather than separating academia into two camps, we should work to establish a more holistic view of scholarship and teaching.

Although we need to be vigorous in reestablishing the importance of teaching at research universities, this does not mean that we should throw the baby out with the bath water by failing to emphasize scholarship. Just because teaching has received short shrift in higher education does not mean that the emphasis on scholarship is to blame. Such a conclusion ignores the adjustments in teaching loads that occur at the four-year level. The real truth, as examined in the opening chapter of this book, is that scholarship can promote better teaching. As any reasonably experienced teacher would be quick to mention, effective teaching is grounded in extensive scholarship.

Yet no matter how clearly we demonstrate the benefits of

scholarship, some of our colleagues will refuse to participate. As any seasoned professor knows, many of our brightest colleagues have grown bitter about the publish or perish approach. Some faculty are resentful that their efforts in the classroom go unnoticed while other less capable teachers receive raises for conducting research. Few in academia would dispute that current administrative practices of rewarding scholarship and ignoring teaching have driven an arbitrary wedge between scholars and teachers. Given the anger and disenchantment felt by our nonpublishing colleagues, we cannot hope that our silent colleagues will join our scholarly discourse if the conditions for teaching are not improved. In addition, because they lack training in writing and publishing, some faculty are unfamiliar with the generative nature of language, of how creative ideas evolve out of scholarly participation, and of how to submit and market their work.

To improve teaching at research universities, we can follow the path taken by Stanford, UCLA, Pennsylvania State University, and the University of South Florida and encourage research universities to develop teaching institutes. However, all of the institutes for faculty development will fail if we do not provide financial incentive for teaching well. As a whole, I think we can agree that few are in academia for the money. Yet at some point mortgages, health care, and even an occasional night on the town are necessary for our spiritual well-being. Unlike the clergy, we did not, after all, take a vow of poverty.

Rather than choosing between scholarship and teaching, we should focus our energies on improving both activities. We can do this by rewarding excellence in the classroom as well as excellence in scholarship. Moreover, as I explore in more detail below, we must redefine scholarship so that it includes practical and pedagogical applications.

HOW CAN WE REDEFINE SCHOLARSHIP?

The popular phrase, "Well, that's academic" is often used to suggest that a subject is superfluous, suitable only for those who have time for leisurely discourse about insignificant issues. Critics of higher education frequently satirize the work of academics in an attempt to make all scholarship seem poorly written and absurdly impractical. For example, Page Smith writes:

The vast majority of the so-called research turned out in the modern university is essentially worthless. It does not result in any measurable benefit to anything or anybody. It does not push back those omnipresent "frontiers of knowledge" so confidently evoked; it does not *in the main* result in greater health or happiness among the general populace or any particular segment of it. It is busywork on a vast, almost incomprehensible scale. It is dispiriting; it depresses the whole scholarly enterprise; and, most important of all, it deprives the student of what he or she deserves—the thoughtful and considerate attention of a teacher deeply and unequivocally committed to teaching; in short, it robs the student of an education. (7)

For us adequately to respond to these important criticisms, we need to do more than improve our writing style. As Ernst Boyer has argued in *Scholarship Reconsidered*, we need to evaluate what we mean by *scholarship* and discuss with our peers and administrators guidelines for rewarding different kinds of scholarship.

Boyer has suggested four primary modes of scholarship: *discovery, integration, application*, and *teaching*. Essentially, *discovery* involves contributing "not only to the stock of human knowledge but also to the intellectual climate of a college or university" (17). *Integration* refers to "making connections across disciplines, placing the specialties in a larger context, illuminating data in a revealing way, often educating nonspecialists" (18). *Application* refers to solving consequential problems, such as heart disease and acid rain. Finally, Boyer notes the interdependence between *teaching* and scholarship and suggests that teaching should be viewed as a form of scholarship since good teachers research their subjects before *transforming* and *extending* knowledge through engendering speculative class discussions and intriguing course materials.

While we certainly should continue rewarding scholarship that aims to *discover* new insights, we should reconsider our tendency to denigrate practical scholarship. After all, extensive research and innovative thinking can be involved in writing a textbook or a pedagogical article, yet these genres traditionally are viewed as inferior to quantitative research. In turn, professors who are able to write well enough to inspire the imaginations of nonspecialists are put down as popularizers or journalists. For example, after receiving the Pulitzer Prize and the Bancroft Award for *The Social Transformation of American Medicine*, Paul Starr was denied tenure and let go from his assistant professor position at Harvard "because he won't publish in the itty bitty academic journals" (Bell, qtd. in Sykes 126). In the *Harvard Crimson* "members of the ad hoc committee" evaluating Starr's application for tenure "sniped that Starr was 'overrated' because he 'merely synthesized old research and presented no new information" (Sykes 127–128).

While we are not privy to the politics at play in this case, the judgment of Starr's tenure committee is not surprising to experienced faculty members: the love affair academics have with "hard research"—that is, quantitative methodologies—is undermining hermeneutical studies, qualitative research, and practical scholarship. While there are no golden tablets that say "thou shalt pursue only original ideas through statistical formulae," the notion that all original scholarship is quantitative is endemic at many research universities. And yet we seriously have not questioned what it takes to be defined as original. To those accustomed to political infighting and the subjective nature of interpretation, it is not surprising that the scholarly community has no well-defined terms for what constitutes an original creation. And while we cannot hope for a rigid definition of what it is to be original, we should do more than shrug our shoulders and say, "I'll know it when I see it; it will be dressed in numbers and fancy jargon." Yes, we can expect increased specialization and use of jargon in our disciplines, but we also need to set aside the absurd assumption that pedagogical and practical articles cannot be original or significant. Many of us fear that our society is collapsing around us. Drugs and violence, the spoiling of the environment, AIDS, the collapse of the schools—these are serious problems that academics should be rewarded for examining. And before giving up on their desire to be of service to our society, academics should study the vitae of those who are calling them popularizers and journalists. Guided by their desire to establish a nationally recognized research institution, many senior scholars apply standards for tenure and promotion that they couldn't hope to achieve.

WHAT CAN THE INSTITUTIONS DO TO ENCOURAGE SCHOLARSHIP?

Many colleges and universities are failing to provide adequate support for faculty. While in the past a few scholars felt impelled to research and publish their ideas, now nearly all academicians at four-year universities are expected to publish to gain tenure, promotion, and respect. Nevertheless, in what amounts to a short-sighted sink-or-swim mentality, most institutions and professional organizations fail to provide the training and social milieu necessary to engender scholarly work. Below I outline some of the changes that we should call for at our institutions to encourage scholarship.

Academic Writers Need to Be Educated about Composition Theory

First, faculty and administrators need to recognize that writing is not a simple, mechanical process. We do not stop learning to write in grammar, middle, or high school, nor should we expect to stop improving as writers after earning our undergraduate and graduate degrees. Instead, writing is an apprenticeship, a lifelong process. Second, we must shatter the assumption that thinking and writing can be separated, that first one thinks and then one writes. Publishing scholars should hold workshops with faculty to help illustrate how the process of writing promotes discovery and creativity.

Faculty Should Be Encouraged to Work Collaboratively

Even though we know that business people work collaboratively to develop better ideas, we tend to expect professors in the humanities and fine arts to write and publish documents by themselves. In fact, when professors do coauthor manuscripts, we tend to frown on their contributions.

Even if faculty choose not to coauthor manuscripts, they still need opportunities to exchange ideas with colleagues in their disciplines as well as other disciplines. Because intradepartmental rivalries can taint the commentary faculty give to each other when exchanging manuscripts, universities and colleges should establish *research institutes* where faculty in different departments and different disciplines can meet to exchange criticisms of each other's projects.

Publishing Scholars Should Receive Financial Support

Scholarship takes tremendous energy. It is blatantly unfair to expect faculty to put in an extra twenty to forty hours a week as researchers if institutions are not prepared to offer rewards for such work. Faculty who are putting in sixty- or seventy-hour weeks, who are struggling to excel as researchers and teachers, deserve compensation and course-load releases. We can assume that the 10 percent of the faculty who are presently active scholars will probably continue writing without compensation, but think about the possible contributions that the nonpublishers might make to our disciplines if institutions recognized their value and rewarded their efforts at scholarly publishing.

In turn, faculty who prefer to teach rather than conduct scholarship should be permitted to teach more and publish less. Yet, given the important benefits of conducting scholarship, even faculty holding teaching contracts at research universities should be expected to write about their teaching goals and pedagogical insights and to make connections to theory in professional journals. Writing is an essential form of thought that should be encouraged.

Institutions Should Attempt to Account for the Quality Rather Than the Quantity of a Scholar's Contributions

Although we lack information about how many articles and books different universities expect from faculty before awarding tenure or promotion, we do know that faculty are under tremendous pressure to publish as much as possible. The pressure to publish voluminously may explain why reports of plagiarism in the *Chronicle of Higher Education* are now so common. Thanks to the pressure to produce quickly, some scholars are taking whole sections from others' work and pawning them off as their own. Other scholars are guilty of fictionalizing their research results.

A more common result of the pressure to publish is the LPU, the *least publishable unit.* To make themselves look productive, faculty will take an idea suitable for one 2,500-word article and carve it into as many vitae lines as possible. Thus a simple pedagogical insight can become the subject of an on-campus presentation, a statewide conference, a national conference, and a brief how-to article, and then be described as a practical implication in the conclusion to a speculative essay.

Assessing the current and potential quality of a scholar's work is a Herculean task. Given the highly specialized nature of most academic work, few academicians have colleagues at their home institutions who are qualified to evaluate their work. Even if qualified critics are available, interpretation is terribly subjective and political infighting is bound to taint the evaluative process. In his entertaining and insightful analysis of why Johann Sebastian Bach would not receive tenure in today's academic climate, Jared Diamond points out a third problem with evaluating a colleague's contributions: academicians in different disciplines tend to mature at different times in their career:

> There are many scholars in fields such as physics and pure mathematics whose brilliant early insights are not matched later in their career. Conversely, scholars in other fields tend to mature later in life. Evolutionary biologists, for instance, have to develop a large body of technical information before they can begin to synthesize their knowledge and their early papers may give few hints of future greatness. The four monographs on barnacle taxonomy that Darwin wrote between the ages of 37 and 45 would have given a university promotions committee little reason to suspect that the same man would publish a truly revolutionary treatise at the age of nearly 51. (100)

Boyer also notes this problem with evaluating the potential of a colleague's work: "Mathematicians and physicists, for example, are most productive in their younger years, while historians and philosophers tend to be most productive later on. Einstein propounded his special theory of relativity at age twenty-six, while Kant's seminal work, *The Critique of Pure Reason*, did not appear until he was fifty-seven" (47).

To be as fair as possible, we need to develop disciplinary-specific standards for tenure and promotion that allow faculty to balance their responsibilities as teachers and researchers. These varied criteria should be public knowledge, and the portfolios that faculty present to illustrate their work as teachers and scholars need to be evaluated by on-campus committee members rather than by a single chairperson. In the best of possible worlds, these portfolios should be sent to qualified colleagues at other institutions as is done when deciding on tenure and promotion. Committee members should be paid for their work and expected to read a sample of each faculty member's work rather than merely scanning the vitae and counting the scholarly documents published. The final report to faculty members should include a completed dichotomous scale that lists all of the pertinent criteria as well as a one-page synthesis.

Institutions Should Fund Frequent Participation at Scholarly Conferences

When faced with financial problems, institutions are often quick to cut funding for travel expenses to scholarly conferences. While it is true that conference presentations usually require less work than publishing in refereed journals, many scholars use conference presentations to try out new ideas, to develop a better sense of audience, to listen in on what the leaders in the field are discussing, and to meet with editors to discuss projects. Institutions that fail to support reasonable travel expenses should not expect significant scholarship or publishing.

Institutions Should Provide Necessary Computer Hardware and Software

Productive faculty should be provided with computers in their offices. To help establish a productive community, faculty should be connected to each other via computer modem.

WHAT CAN PROFESSIONAL ORGANIZATIONS DO TO PROMOTE SCHOLARSHIP?

The Peer-Review System Must Be Improved

Because people's careers are often determined by what they publish, we should be troubled by recent research suggesting that reviewers' decisions to accept articles or fund grants are often arbitrary or political.

Interpretation will always be subjective, yet we should look into ways to make it more objective. Professional organizations and journal editors need to examine how reviewers for manuscripts are selected and how they make decisions. Perhaps journal editors can work with their reviewers to standardize the criteria used by reviewers to evaluate manuscripts. Meanwhile, we should act on what we know and make the following changes:

1. Scholars should not be expected to wait longer than three months to hear whether their submissions are accepted or rejected. Current practices of expecting academicians to wait a year or longer to hear whether an essay is accepted are unconscionable.

2. The submissions should be blind—that is, the author's name and institution should not be made known to the reviewers. The star system should be abandoned so that new voices can enter the conversation.

3. As an acknowledgment of their efforts, reviewers should receive an honorarium, even if it's a minor one such as a free journal subscription.

The Variations in Documentation Styles and Descriptors for Computerized Databases Should Be Ditched

It is simply ludicrous to have so many different formats for documenting sources. These variations cause needless busywork. Professional organizations should agree on one or two dominant ways of citing sources. Likewise, we need to encourage the producers of on-line and CD-ROM databases to use one standard list of descriptors.

Professional Organizations Should Work to Clarify the Standards for "Fair Usage" and to Make Permission Fees More Reasonable

Some important books are not publishable because of excessive permission fees. It is nearly impossible, for example, to publish a book that analyzes contemporary song lyrics. It can also be impossible to publish a collection of reprinted scholarly articles because the journals in which the articles were originally published require high reprint fees. Considering that the authors of scholarly essays often receive little or no compensation for their manuscripts when originally published, the demand for high reprint fees seems unfair. Professional organizations need to work with publishers and producers of songs, films, cartoons, and the like to help them better understand the economics and goals of scholarly publishing.

WHAT CAN FACULTY DO TO PROMOTE SCHOLARSHIP?

Faculty Should Stop Signing Their Rights Away

Desperate to publish to gain tenure or promotion, academicians agree to pay part of the costs of publishing; they prepare documents in camera-ready format; they give up royalties or accept ridiculously low ones; and, worst of all, they give copyright to the publisher. As discussed in the chapter on writing book proposals, *acceptability conditions* and *assignment conditions*, which publishers are quick to call standard boilerplate, skew their contracts to enslave academicians.

Yet what can we realistically do? In "A Writer's Union for Academics?," Stanley Aronowitz has argued persuasively that we should join the National Writers Union, which "was established in 1983 to organize writers to bargain with their employers—including book publishers, periodicals, and companies contracting with a wide variety of freelance technical and PR writers" (43). Likewise, in "Composition Textbooks: Publisher-Author Relationships," W. Ross Winterowd suggests that academicians can escape enslavement by "joining the Textbook Authors Association (founded by Mike Keedy, Purdue professor emeritus of mathematics), which held its first meeting in December of 1987" (146).

If we are ever to get a taste of the $147.8 million brought in from university press sales (Aronowitz 41) and the billions that textbook publishers bring in, we will need to speak as a group and demand more equitable contracts. Otherwise, we will remain trapped by a system that perpetuates enslavement and poverty.

FINAL COMMENTS

Writing can be an invigorating way of engaging the imagination, of learning, and of staying intellectually alive. As Boyer has argued, we need to encourage and reward scholarship that discovers, integrates, applies, and extends knowledge. Yet we cannot expect our silent colleagues to join and enrich our scholarly conversations if we do not tackle the serious problems undermining higher education.

Many faculty members have grown embittered about the emphasis on scholarship. We have been accused of abandoning the classroom and of pursuing narrow, relatively insignificant subjects in a blind pursuit of "original knowledge." While conveniently ignoring the adjustments research universities make to the teaching loads of faculty members, numerous critics have ridiculed contemporary scholarship as indecipherable busywork. In part these criticisms are justified. Current ways of evaluating scholars emphasize quantity over quality. And the importance of teaching has been undermined by our lack of willingness to assess it or reward it. As scholars and teachers, we need to step out of the classroom and address these criticisms. We need to let administrators and legislators know more about our pedagogical and scholarly efforts. We need to educate those blinded by the limitations of dualistic or even egocentric thought. We must drive a stake into the heart of the scholarship versus teaching debate. We must recognize that some academicians are fine scholars even if they are reluctant writers. After all, we all know people who read widely and freely share their insights with colleagues and students. We must embrace applied forms of scholarship, philosophical and historical treatments, and qualitative methods (such as ethnography and case study). We need to take a hard look at our use of jargon in technical articles. And we need to reach out in our writing to our colleagues in other disciplines and to interested people in general.

In short, we need to clean house, And this means that we need you to write, to share your voice with us. Help us tackle the problems now corroding the foundation of higher education.

WORKS CITED

Aronowitz, Stanley. "A Writer's Union for Academics?" *Thought and Action: The NEA Higher Education Journal* 4:2 (Fall 1988): 41–46.

Boyer, Ernst. *Scholarship Reconsidered: Priorities of the Professoriate.* Princeton, N.J.: Carnegie Foundation for the Advancement of Teaching, 1990.

Diamond, Jared. "Publish or Perish." *Discover* (July 1989): 96–101.

Smith, Page. *Killing the Spirit: Higher Education in America.* New York: Viking, 1990.

Sykes, Charles J. *ProfScam: Professors and the Demise of Higher Education.* Washington, D.C.: Regnery Gateway, 1988.

Winterowd, W. Ross. "Composition Textbooks: Publisher-Author Relationships." *College Composition and Communication* 40 (May 1989): 139–151.

Selected Bibliography

GENERAL INFORMATION SOURCES FOR ACADEMIC WRITERS

Association of American University Presses Directory. New York: AAUP (Association of American University Presses), annual.

Katz, Bill, and Linda Sternberg Katz, eds. *Magazines for Libraries*. 6th ed. New York: Bowker, 1989.

Koester, Jane, and Bruce Hillman, eds. *Writer's Market*. Cincinnati: Writer's Digest Books, annual.

Lingua Franca: The Review of Academic Life. Mamaroneck, N.Y.: Lingua Franca, bimonthly.

Literary Market Place. New York: Bowker, annual.

Standard Periodical Directory. New York: Oxbridge, annual.

Ulrich's International Periodicals Directory. New York: Bowker, annual.

GENERAL INFORMATION ABOUT ACADEMIC WRITING, POLITICS, AND SCHOLARLY PUBLISHING

Academic Publishing Journal. Lincoln, Nebr.: Theraplan, quarterly.

Boyer, Ernst. *Scholarship Reconsidered: Priorities of the Professoriate.* Princeton, N.J.: Carnegie Foundation for the Advancement of Teaching, 1990.

Parsons, Paul. *Getting Published: The Acquisition Process at University Presses.* Knoxville: University of Tennessee Press, 1989.

Scholarly Publishing. Toronto: University of Toronto Press, quarterly.

Smith, Page. *Killing the Spirit: Higher Education in America.* New York: Viking, 1990.

Sykes, Charles J. *ProfScam: Professors and the Demise of Higher Education.* Washington, D.C.: Regnery Gateway, 1988.

PROPOSALS—WRITING THEM AND FINDING FUNDING SOURCES

Annual Register of Grant Support. Chicago: Marquis Academy Media, annual.

Foundation Center. *Corporate Foundation Profiles.* 7th ed. New York: Foundation Center, 1992.

———. *The Foundation Directory.* 1992 ed. New York: Foundation Center, annual.

———. *The Foundation Directory Supplement.* New York: Foundation Center, 1992.

———. *The Foundation Directory Part 2.* 1991/1992 ed. New York: Foundation Center, annual.

———. *Foundation 1000.* 1992 ed. New York: Foundation Center, annual.

———. *Grant Guides.* 1991/92 ed. New York: Foundation Center, 1992.

———. *The National Directory of Corporate Giving.* 2nd ed. New York: Foundation Center, 1991.

———. *National Data Book of Foundations.* 1992 ed. New York: Foundation Center, 1992.

Park, Karin R., and Beth Luey. *Publication Grants for Writers and Publishers.* Phoenix: Oryx Press, 1991.

Schumacher, Dorin. *Get Funded! A Practical Guide for Scholars Seeking Research Support from Business.* Newbury Park, Calif.: Sage Publications, 1992.

Taft Group. *1991 Taft Foundation Reporter.* Rockville, Md.: Taft Group, 1991.

White, Virginia, ed. *Grant Proposals That Succeeded.* New York: Plenum Press, 1984.

SUBJECT AREA GUIDES

This section lists some of the most prominent guides to academic journals and scholarly presses in the fields of business and economics, education, health and medicine, the humanities, library and information science, social and behavioral sciences, and technology and science. Most of these guides offer information about the submission and editorial policies of the journals referenced in them. Because editors of scholarly journals frequently serve short terms, however, you should check a specific periodical for the current editor's name and address.

If you work in a very specialized area, consult your professional association to determine whether a guide is available for your subject area. (If none is available, consider putting one together.)

Business and Economics

Cabell, David, ed. *Directory of Publishing Opportunities in Business and Economics.* 4th ed. Beaumont, Tex.: Cabell, 1988.

Fisher, William, comp. *Financial Journals and Serials: An Analytical Guide to Accounting, Banking, Finance, Insurance, and Investment Periodicals.* Annotated Bibliographies of Serials: A Subject Approach Series. Westport, Conn.: Greenwood Press, 1986.

Miller, A. Carolyn, and Victoria J. Punsalan, comps. *Refereed and Nonrefereed Economic Journals: A Guide to Publishing Opportunities.* Westport, Conn.: Greenwood Press, 1988.

Sichel, Beatrice, and Werner Sichel, comps. *Economics Journals and Serials: An Analytical Guide.* Annotated Bibliographies of Serials: A Subject Approach Series. Westport, Conn.: Greenwood Press, 1986.

Vargo, Richard J. *The Author's Guide to Accounting and Financial Reporting Publications.* Rev. ed. New York: Harper, 1986.

Vocino, Michael C., comp. *Labor and Industrial Relations Journals and Serials: An Analytical Guide.* Annotated Bibliographies of Serials: A Subject Approach Series. Westport, Conn.: Greenwood Press, 1989

Education

Cabell, David, ed. *Directory of Publishing Opportunities in Education.* 2 vols. Beaumont, Tex.: Cabell, 1989.

Collins, Mary Ellen, comp. *Education Journals and Serials: An Analytical Guide.* Annotated Bibliographies of Serials: A Subject Approach Series. Westport, Conn.: Greenwood Press, 1988.

Judy, Stephen N., ed. *Publishing in English Education.* Montclair, N.J.: Boynton Cook, 1982.

Levin, Joel. *Getting Published: The Educator's Resource Book*. New York: ARCO, 1983.
Manera, Elizabeth S., and Robert Wright. *Annotated Writer's Guide to Professional Journals*. Scottsdale, Ariz.: Bobets, 1982.
Silverman, Robert J. *Getting Published in Education Journals*. Springfield, Ill.: Thomas, 1982.

Health and Medicine

Barnes, Joan, comp. *The Medical and Scientific Author's Guide: An International Reference Guide for Authors to More than 500 Medical and Scientific Journals*. New York: Le Jacq, 1984.
Hesslein, Shirley B., comp. *Serials on Aging: An Analytical Guide*. Annotated Bibliographies of Serials: A Subject Approach Series. Westport, Conn.: Greenwood Press, 1986.
Kowitz, Aletha, comp. *Dentistry Journals and Serials: An Analytical Guide*. Annotated Bibliographies of Serials: A Subject Approach Series. Westport, Conn.: Greenwood Press, 1988.
Vaillancourt, Pauline M., comp. *Cancer Journals and Serials: An Analytical Guide*. Annotated Bibliographies of Serials: A Subject Approach Series. Westport, Conn.: Greenwood Press, 1988.
Warner, Steven D., and Kathryn D. Schweer. *Author's Guide to Journals in Nursing and Related Fields*. Author's Guide to Journals Series. New York: Haworth, 1982.

The Humanities

Dawsey, James M. *Scholar's Guide to Academic Journals in Religion*. Metuchen, N.J.: Scarecrow Press, 1988.
Fieg, Eugene C., Jr., comp. *Religion Journals and Serials: An Analytical Guide*. Annotated Bibliographies of Serials: A Subject Approach Series. Westport, Conn.: Greenwood Press, 1988.
Harner, James L. *MLA Directory of Scholarly Presses*. New York: MLA, 1992.
Kent, Kathleen L., comp. *MLA Directory of Periodicals: A Guide to Journals and Series in Languages and Literatures*. New York: MLA, biennial.
Ruben, Douglas H., comp. *Philosophy Journals and Serials: An Analytical Guide*. Annotated Bibliographies of Serials: A Subject Approach Series. Westport, Conn.: Greenwood Press, 1985.

Library and Information Sciences

Alley, Brian, and Jennifer Cargill. *Librarian in Search of a Publisher: How to Get Published.* Phoenix: Oryx Press, 1986.

Bowman, Mary Ann, comp. *Library and Information Science Journals and Serials: An Analytical Guide.* Annotated Bibliographies of Serials: A Subject Approach Series. Westport, Conn.: Greenwood Press, 1985.

Stevens, Norman D., and Nora B. Stevens, eds. *Author's Guide to Journals in Library and Information Science.* Author's Guide to Journals Series. New York: Haworth, 1982.

Social and Behavioral Sciences

Fyfe, Janet, comp. *History Journals and Serials: An Analytical Guide.* Annotated Bibliographies of Serials: A Subject Approach Series. Westport, Conn.: Greenwood Press, 1986.

Mendelsohn, Henry N. *An Author's Guide to Social Work Journals.* 2nd ed. Silver Spring, Md.: National Association of Social Workers, 1987.

Wang, Alvin Y. *Author's Guide to Journals in the Behavioral Sciences.* Hillsdale, N.J.: Erlbaum Associates, 1989.

Williams, John T., comp. *Anthropology Journals and Serials: An Analytical Guide.* Annotated Bibliographies of Serials: A Subject Approach Series. Westport, Conn.: Greenwood Press, 1986.

Technology and Science

Balachandran, Sarojini. *Directory of Publishing Sources: The Researcher's Guide to Journals in Engineering and Technology.* New York: Wiley-Interscience, 1982.

Barnett, Judith B., comp. *Marine Science Journals and Serials: An Analytical Guide.* Annotated Bibliographies of Serials: A Subject Approach Series. Westport, Conn.: Greenwood Press, 1986.

Jensen, Richard D., Connie Lamb, and Nathan M. Smith, comps. *Agricultural and Animal Sciences Journals and Serials: An Analytical Guide.* Annotated Bibliographies of Serials: A Subject Approach Series. Westport, Conn.: Greenwood Press, 1986.

WRITING AND STYLE MANUALS

American Psychological Association. *Publication Manual of the American Psychological Association.* 3rd ed. Washington, D.C.: APA, 1983.

Boice, Robert. *Professors as Writers: A Self-Help Guide to Productive Writing.* Stillwater, Okla.: New Forums Press, 1990.

Chicago Manual of Style. 13th ed. Chicago: University of Chicago Press, 1982.

Cook, Claire Kehrwald. *Line by Line: How to Improve Your Own Writing.* New York: MLA, 1985.

Day, Robert A. *How to Write and Publish a Scientific Paper.* 3rd ed. Phoenix: Oryx Press, 1988.

Elbow, Peter. *Writing Without Teachers.* London: Oxford University Press, 1973.

Fox, Mary Frank. *Scholarly Writing & Publishing: Issues, Problems, and Solutions.* Boulder: Westview Press, 1985.

Gibaldi, Joseph, and Walter S. Achtert. *MLA Handbook for Writers of Research Papers.* New York: Modern Language Association, 1988.

Luey, Beth. *Handbook for Academic Authors.* Cambridge: Cambridge University Press, 1989.

Michaelson, Herbert B. *How to Write and Publish Engineering Papers and Reports.* 3rd ed. Phoenix: Oryx Press, 1990.

Moxley, Joseph M., ed. *Writing and Publishing for Academic Authors.* Lanham, Md.: University Press of America, 1992.

Strunk, William, Jr., and E. B. White. *The Elements of Style.* 3rd ed. New York: Macmillan, 1979.

vanLeunen, Mary-Claire. *A Handbook for Scholars, Revised Edition.* New York: Oxford University Press, 1992.

Williams, Joseph M. *Style: Ten Lessons in Clarity and Grace.* 2nd ed. Glenview, Ill.: Scott, Foresman and Co., 1985.

Zinsser, William. *On Writing Well.* 3rd ed. New York: Harper and Row, 1985.

Index

About the Author

JOSEPH M. MOXLEY is Associate Professor of English at the University of South Florida, Tampa. He teaches graduate and undergraduate courses in composition theory and related subjects and also conducts writing seminars for university faculty. The author of many scholarly articles and book chapters on aspects of writing, as well as published fiction and poetry, his books include *Creative Writing in America: Theory and Pedagogy* and a composition text, *Eureka: Writers at Work*. Moxley has also served in various editorial capacities on the *Journal of Advanced Composition*, *Technical Communication*, and other academic journals.